This compelling message is an alarm clock waking believers from their stupor. Read it soon.

—Gov. Mike Huckabee

Dr. Youssef has been on my show discussing the Islamist agenda. In *Jesus, Jihad, and Peace*, he goes much deeper, answering questions we all have about today's turbulent events in the Middle East and what they mean in prophetic terms.

—Sean Hannity
Host, *Hannity*, Fox News

JESUS, JIHAD ⸺ AND ⸺ PEACE

WHAT BIBLE PROPHECY SAYS
ABOUT WORLD EVENTS TODAY

JESUS, JIHAD AND PEACE

WHAT BIBLE PROPHECY SAYS
ABOUT WORLD EVENTS TODAY

MICHAEL YOUSSEF

WORTHY®
PUBLISHING

Copyright © 2015 by Michael Youssef

Published by Worthy Books, an imprint of Worthy Publishing Group, a division of Worthy Media, Inc., 134 Franklin Road, Suite 200, Brentwood, Tennessee 37027.

WORTHY is a registered trademark of Worthy Media, Inc.

HELPING PEOPLE EXPERIENCE THE HEART OF GOD

eBook available wherever digital books are sold.

Library of Congress Cataloging-in-Publication Data

Youssef, Michael.
  Jesus, Jihad, and peace : what does Bible prophecy say about world events today? / by Michael Youssef, Ph.D.
    pages cm
  Includes bibliographical references.
  ISBN 978-1-61795-368-2 (tradepaper)
  1. Bible--Prophecies--End of the world. 2. Christianity and other religions--
Islam. 3. Islam--Relations--
Christianity. I. Title.
  BS649.E63Y685 2015
  220.1'5--dc23

                                                                    2014030897

Unless otherwise noted, all Scripture quotations are taken from The Holy Bible, New International Version®, NIV® Copyright © 1973, 1978, 1984, 2011 by Biblica, Inc.® Used by permission. All rights reserved worldwide.

Scripture quotations marked KJV are taken from the King James Version of the Bible. Public domain.

All quotations from the Koran are taken from the Abdullah Yusuf Ali translation in *Three Translations of The Koran (Al-Qur'an) Side by Side* (in the public domain) at http://www.gutenberg.org/cache/epub/16955/pg16955.html.

For foreign and subsidiary rights, contact rights@worthypublishing.com

Published in association with Don Gates, The Gates Group, www.the-gates-group.com

ISBN: 978-1-61795-368-2

Cover Design: Smartt Guys design

Interior Design and Typesetting: Christopher D. Hudson & Associates, Inc.

Printed in the United States of America

15 16 17 18 19 VPI 8 7 6 5 4 3 2 1

To Dale Sostad,
whose obedience to the Lord
made it possible for millions of people to hear the gospel,
some for the first time,
and be set free from Satan's clutches.

Contents

Author's Preface

I WAS BORN IN THE MIDDLE EAST, spent my early years in the culture of the Middle East, and I return to the Middle East often. I have had many long, revealing conversations with Muslims in general and Islamist hard-liners in particular. I know the Middle East well and have had much firsthand experience with Islamic practices and thought processes. Although I am an American now, for most of my life I have lived with one foot in the West and one foot in the East.

Throughout this book, I have tried to distinguish between Islamic ideology and Muslims as people. I have many dear friends and acquaintances who embrace Islam. While I risk being criticized for my sociological, economic, political, and religious assessments of Islam, my ardent desire is that no one would misunderstand my genuine affection and appreciation for Muslim people.

From my perspective as a Christian, I see all other religious systems as less than whole. Jesus declared, "I am the way and the truth and the life. No one comes to the Father except through me" (John 14:6). And the apostle Peter testified before the members of the Jewish ruling council, the Sanhedrin, "Salvation is found in no one else, for there is no other name under heaven given to mankind by which we must be saved" (Acts 4:12). I cannot be true to my Christian faith and believe otherwise.

Yet the fact that I, as a Christian, understand Islam to be a false worldview does not mean I look down on Muslim people in any way. On the contrary, I am compelled by my love for Muslim people. I feel a deep burden for them, and I humbly yearn for them to know the fullness of life that comes only through a personal relationship with Jesus Christ.

A Wake-Up Call

AL-QAEDA FOUNDER OSAMA BIN LADEN was killed by Navy SEALs at his compound in Abbottabad, Pakistan, on May 2, 2011. Almost five months later, Anwar al-Awlaki, one of al-Qaeda's top recruiters, was killed by a CIA drone attack in Yemen. Yet the threat of terrorism only grew greater and more frightening in the ensuing months.

By 2014, we began to hear rumblings of a new terror threat in the Middle East. Operating for years beneath the radar of Western news organizations, a Sunni terror group called "al-Qaeda in Iraq" broke away from the larger al-Qaeda organization. Calling itself the Islamic State of Iraq and Syria (ISIS) or the Islamic State of Iraq and the Levant (ISIL) or simply the Islamic State (IS), it proclaimed itself a caliphate, with religious authority over all Muslims.

ISIS took advantage of the civil war in Syria and the power vacuum in Iraq following the US departure. It metastasized like a cancer, swallowing territory, conquering villages and cities (including Mosul, the second-largest city in Iraq), slaughtering thousands of Christians and Shiite Muslims, and dumping their bodies in mass graves. In August 2014, the *Wall Street Journal* reported that ISIS was running a self-sustaining economy by looting banks, selling pirated oil and antiquities, ransoming kidnap victims, and extorting protection money from business owners, farmers, Christians, and other religious minorities.[1]

We are horrified at the inhuman acts of ISIS—from beheading journalists to crucifying, stoning, and beheading Christian men, women, and children.[2] We turn away from these horrors, wishing we could get the images out of our minds, feeling sorry for "those poor people over there," and feeling glad that "at least that could never happen here."

Yet if ISIS and other Islamist groups get their way, they *will* bring these horrors here. They won't stop at gobbling up Iraq and Syria or the entire Middle East or Europe and Africa. Their goal is to establish a *global* Caliphate. Could ISIS accomplish this ambitious goal? Who knows?

But no one should assume that Western civilization is safe. No one should assume that ISIS cannot do what it says it will do. In January 2014, ISIS controlled one city—Fallujah, forty-three miles west of Baghdad. By August 2014, ISIS controlled one-third of Iraq and one-third of Syria, and it showed no signs of stopping. No one can predict what the forces of Islamic extremism might accomplish.

So we wonder, What's next? Is there any hope for world peace—or is terror our destiny? Why is there so much turmoil in the Middle East? How can we understand the mind-set of

Islamic extremists whose ideology is so fanatical that they are willing to kill themselves in order to slaughter us?

Bible-believing Christians have even more questions: How does radical Islam fit into Bible prophecy? What do today's turbulent events in Israel, Palestine, Egypt, Syria, Iran (biblical Persia), Iraq (biblical Babylon), and Russia (biblical Magog) mean in prophetic terms? In a world that is crying out for peace, which will prevail: Jesus or jihad?

Christians and non-Christians alike look at alarming developments in the Middle East and around the globe and wonder what the implications are for our future. Judaism, Christianity, and Islam feature parallel accounts of the end times, and all three accounts focus on a messianic Savior, an apocalyptic final war between good and evil, and a central role for the city of Jerusalem. Do these prophetic end-times scenarios intersect in some way? And, more pressingly, do recent global events reveal that we are living in the end times?

It has never been more important to understand Bible prophecy in relation to world events. If we spread out today's headlines alongside the prophecies of God's Word, we notice many disturbing parallels. We see that prophecies written centuries before Christ still cast their shadows over the twenty-first century. The warnings Jesus issued on the Mount of Olives are frighteningly relevant today.

In this book, I will shed light on the ideology and events in the Middle East with answers that are concise, biblically accurate, and targeted on the challenges that confront us in this dangerous world. Westerners in general, and Christians in particular, are the targets of Islamic extremist terror attacks. So we seek to understand who is attacking us, how these trends fit into the flow of prophecy, and how we should respond.

Jesus, Jihad, and Peace is not a pop-theology book exploiting end-times mania. Instead, this book looks at current events against the backdrop of biblical prophecy and issues a clarion call: Wake up! Heed the warnings of Scripture and read the prophetic signs all around you!

Just as in Old Testament times, God is displaying His character and His purpose through global events. This book unmasks the intentions of Islamic extremism, exposes the threat that radical Islam poses to the free world, and calls us to turn back to Jesus—before it's too late.

ONE

The Goal of
World Domination

$\mathbf{M}$OHAMED BOUAZIZI WAS a twenty-six-year-old street vendor in Sidi Bouzid, a rural village in central Tunisia. His father died when he was three, and his stepfather was unable to work. So from the time he was ten, Mohamed had worked hard to provide for his family. In his twenties, he found it difficult to find work and was rejected by the army, so he bought a vendor's cart and sold produce, earning a little more than a hundred dollars a month. He budgeted his money carefully so that he could help support his mother, stepfather, and siblings. He even put one sister through college. He also set a little money aside each month in hopes of one day replacing his cart with a van.[1]

His customers loved him. "Mohamed was a very well-known and popular man," said a friend, Hajlaoui Jaafer. "He would give free fruit and vegetables to very poor families." Yet Mohamed was constantly bullied by the police, who demanded bribes and confiscated his produce when he couldn't pay. "Since he was a child, they were mistreating him," said Jaafer.[2]

On the morning of December 17, 2010, as Mohamed Bouazizi was on the street, selling his wares, the police stopped him to shake him down for another bribe. Not only did Mohamed have no money for a bribe, but he had borrowed two hundred dollars to buy produce for his cart. When Mohamed said he couldn't pay the bribe, a woman named Faida Hamdy, a municipal official, came out to confront him. Witnesses say she confiscated Mohamed's weighing scales (valued at one hundred dollars), and when he protested, she slapped him, spat at him, insulted his dead father, and overturned his produce cart. In Mohamed's culture, being shamed by a woman is the ultimate humiliation.

With his produce ruined, how could he pay back the loan? The police told Mohamed he would be fined, but he had no money to pay the fine. He went to the governor's office to ask for his scales back, but the governor refused to see him. Believing his life was ruined, Mohamed stood in the intersection in front of the governor's office, doused himself with gasoline, and shouted, "How do you expect me to make a living?"[3]

Then he flicked a match and set himself ablaze.

Severely burned over 90 percent of his body, he lived for eighteen days in the hospital and then died on January 4, 2011. More than five thousand people attended Mohamed Bouazizi's funeral, enraged that the corrupt government had destroyed the twenty-six-year-old street vendor's hope.[4]

Anti-government anger spread through the country like wildfire. People expressed their rage through mass demonstrations and revolts from one end of Tunisia to the other, sending Tunisian president Zine Ben Ali fleeing into exile in Saudi Arabia.

The spark of revolution spread quickly across the region. In Egypt, thousands of protesters poured into historic Tahrir (Liberation) Square in Cairo. Protests also popped up in Alexandria, Suez, and other Egyptian cities. The demonstrations were nonviolent at the beginning, but as the government of Egyptian president Hosni Mubarak clamped down, clashes broke out, killing hundreds and injuring thousands. Demonstrators demanded an end to the corrupt, repressive Mubarak regime. On February 11, 2011, after eighteen days of protests and violence, Hosni Mubarak resigned, ending three decades of the Egyptian police state.

More civil uprisings took place in Bahrain, Yemen, Oman, Algeria, Jordan, Syria, Iraq, Morocco, Kuwait, Lebanon, Mauritania, Saudi Arabia, Sudan, and Western Sahara. Palestinian protesters launched demonstrations along the borders of Israel. Jordan, Kuwait, Lebanon, Oman, and Morocco implemented reforms to prevent the protests from getting out of control. A full-fledged civil war broke out in Libya, which sent Libyan dictator Muammar Gaddafi scurrying for cover. On October 20, 2011, NATO planes struck a convoy of vehicles. Gaddafi, who was in one of the vehicles, escaped and hid in a drainpipe. Libyan rebels dragged him out of the drain, beat him, and dealt him a brutal tyrant's death.

The Syrian government, by contrast, doubled its repressive measures and eventually resorted to chemical weapons.

In country after country across the Arab world, people chanted, *"El Shaab yurid iskat el Nizam!"* (The people want the fall of the regime!)[5] Thus began a wave of uprisings that came to be known as the "Arab Spring."

The False Hope of the Arab Spring

In the early stages of the Egyptian uprisings, there was cooperation between Egyptian Christians and Muslims. For example, after a New Year's Day 2011 car bomb destroyed the Saints Church in east Alexandria, killing twenty-five worshippers, Muslims attended Mass alongside the Coptic Christians as a show of support. One Muslim Egyptian told the *Los Angeles Times*, "I'm here to tell all my Coptic brothers that Muslims and Christians are an inseparable pillar of Egypt's texture. . . . We will share any pains or threats they go through."[6]

Initially, that spirit of cooperation flowed both ways. In February 2011, as anti-Mubarak demonstrations were in full swing in Cairo, thousands of Muslims gathered in Tahrir Square to protest and pray. Hundreds of Coptic Christians encircled their Muslim compatriots, joining hands to form a protective cordon around the Muslims against police and military forces.[7] But just a month later, as the BBC reported, Tahrir Square became the site of violent clashes between Christians and Muslims, killing thirteen people.[8]

Across Egypt, cooperation between Christians and Muslims disintegrated and clashes erupted. In late February 2011, a

Coptic priest was stabbed to death by masked men shouting, "Allah is great!"[9] On March 12, the Shahedin Church in Helwan Province was torched by a Muslim mob, setting off a street battle that killed thirteen Christians.[10] In May, a dozen Egyptians were killed in attacks on Coptic churches.[11] On September 20, a Muslim mob partially destroyed the al-Marenab Church in the southern Aswan Province.[12]

Though many young Muslims demonstrated support and solidarity with Christians in Egypt, the Muslim extremists and hard-liners infiltrated the Arab Spring movement and turned it into an opportunity to terrorize and kill Christians.

For example, Ayman Anwar Mitri is a Coptic Christian, a middle-aged man living in the Egyptian town of Qena. Mitri rented an apartment he owned to two Muslim sisters. In early 2011, soon after the beginning of the Arab Spring uprisings, Mitri learned that the two sisters had been charged with prostitution. Not wanting his property used for immoral purposes, he evicted the women.

Days later, Mitri was awakened at four in the morning by a phone call telling him the apartment was on fire. He arrived as firemen were extinguishing the blaze. As Mitri inspected the damage, a Muslim appeared at the door, tricked him into going to another apartment—and there a dozen Muslim men ambushed him and began beating him. The fire had been a setup to lure Mitri into a trap. The Muslim men shouted, "We will teach you a lesson, Christian!" The group brought in one of the sisters and ordered her to admit an adulterous relationship with Mitri. She refused, so they beat her until she accused Mitri.

The Muslims hacked off Mitri's right ear, gashed the back of his neck, and slit his other ear and his arms. They were about to toss Mitri out of the window of the fifth-floor apartment when a policeman among them said killing Mitri would get them into trouble. The men demanded that Mitri convert to Islam, but he refused. Finally, the men called the police, who came and took Mitri and the prostitute away. No one was ever arrested for the attack on Ayman Mitri.[13]

The Arab Spring in Egypt began as a pro-democracy movement under the slogan, "The people want the fall of the regime!" Yet the young pro-democracy reformers who had set the Arab Spring into motion were leaderless and disorganized. So Islamic hard-liners quickly seized these demonstrations for their own purposes. Before it was over, gangs of Muslim men swarmed through Cairo with clubs and torches, chanting, "The people want to bring down the Christians!"[14] I personally spoke with Christian leaders in Cairo, and they told of roving gangs of thugs who smashed and looted shops and banks.

An Egyptian-Canadian friend told me she had gotten through to her family and learned that her father was sick and bleeding in the hospital, but most of the medical staff had fled so there was no one left to provide medical care. The janitor and other low-level hospital workers defended the patients from thugs and looters. It was anarchy, and the police could not protect the citizens.

While Western news agencies painted a rosy picture of the Arab Spring as a peaceful outbreak of pro-democracy feelings, the Arab Spring movement was co-opted by Islamic fundamentalists, including <u>the Salafi sect (followers of the</u> <u>Salafiyyah Islamic movement), which views mob violence as</u> <u>a legitimate form of Sharia justice. *Sharia* literally means "the</u> <u>straight path," and Muslims believe that Sharia law governs</u> <u>all aspects of life.</u>

<u>The hope of the Arab Spring proved to be a mirage.</u>

The Pattern of Islamic Revolution

During the early stages of the uprisings, I accepted invitations to appear on CNN, Fox News, the Christian Broadcasting Network, and other news outlets to talk about these events. While most Western media celebrated this seeming wave of freedom sweeping the Arab world, I was one of the few voices sounding a warning. I predicted these changes would result in violence and persecution for Christians—and as Muslim mobs torched Egyptian churches and Egyptian military vehicles rolled into crowds of peaceful Christian demonstrators, my predictions came to pass.

Appearing on Governor Mike Huckabee's show on Fox News Channel, I said, "I'm not here to defend former president Hosni Mubarak. During his thirty-year tenure, state corruption grew and political dissidents were often imprisoned without trial. At the same time, Mubarak made a number of positive reforms. For example, he privatized the banks and grew the economy, which in turn helped create a large Egyptian middle class."

In 2011, I saw student protesters waving signs that read, "Down with the tyrant Mubarak!" I thought, *Those kids don't know what a real tyrant is.* I grew up in Egypt under the harsh rule of Gamal Abdel Nasser. When I was around my friends in high school, I avoided talking about politics because I never knew which of my friends might be a government informant. It seemed like every other person was a potential informant, and every once in a while, someone you knew would be denounced and arrested. It was like living in George Orwell's *1984*. Life under Mubarak was no utopia, but it was hardly the repressive Egyptian society I grew up in.

The young, university-educated demonstrators of the Arab Spring were sincere in their desire for freedom and democracy. But they didn't realize that Islamic extremists were working in the shadows, exploiting their youthful fervor and quietly infiltrating and manipulating the revolution, just as Ayatollah Khomeini had manipulated the Iranian Revolution more than three decades earlier.

During the Iranian Revolution of 1979, Islamists stirred up revolutionary passions and sent students into the streets of Tehran to demonstrate against Mohammad Reza Shah Pahlavi. When the Shah abdicated and left the country, Ayatollah Khomeini took over the revolution. All the freedom-loving protesters who dreamed of a democratic Iran were silenced. The last thing Islamists want for the people is freedom.

That's the pattern most Arab world revolutions follow. Hidden Islamists stir the pot and keep idealistic students inflamed and angry. Once the revolution is in full swing, the Islamists seize power, round up the activists, and chop off their heads—either figuratively or literally. After the revolution, the Islamists refer to the original demonstrators as *hemir al-thawra* (donkeys of the revolution)—stooges to be used and then discarded.

Hamas, the Sunni Palestinian terror organization and political party, followed the same pattern in coming to power in the Gaza Strip. An offshoot of Egypt's Muslim Brotherhood, Hamas gained power by exploiting the revolutionary passions of the demonstrators during the First Intifada, the Palestinian uprising against Israel in 1987.

And the same pattern has been playing out in Egypt. As I told Governor Huckabee, "If the Egyptian political system falls, it will be a free-for-all. The extremists and militants will move in for the kill. Make no mistake, they will use the secular-educated Muslims to get the power, but once they get to power, they are going to get the dissidents out of the way. . . . Their number-one goal is to break the accord with Israel, create an alliance with Hamas in Gaza, and then reignite the conflict and enmity with Israel again. . . . The Arab world is in ferment all around the nation of Israel and is working all around the borders of Israel. Once Israel falls, their vision, their third wave of jihad, is Europe and then the United States."

Islamic extremists are totally committed to their goal of establishing a global Muslim state, the Caliphate (more on that in chapter 8).

The Muslim Brotherhood

One of the largest and most influential of all the Islamic extremist groups is the Muslim Brotherhood. The Muslim

Brotherhood, founded in Egypt in 1928, now operates throughout the world, including the United States. The slogan of the Muslim Brotherhood is "Islam is the solution." The credo of the Brotherhood is "Allah is our objective. The Prophet is our leader. Koran is our law. Jihad is our way. Dying in the way of Allah is our highest hope."[15]

Where did the Muslim Brotherhood come from and what are its goals for the Arab world? What are its goals for the West?

The Muslim Brotherhood was founded in 1928 by a schoolteacher named Hasan al-Banna. He was angry and frustrated over Western political influence and the declining influence of Islam in Egypt. He had two goals in mind when he founded the Brotherhood. His short-term goal was the expulsion of the British from Egypt. His long-term goal was to establish the Caliphate, a global Muslim state with the Koran as its only constitution. A brief review of history will show how Hasan al-Banna became such an influential figure in the Islamic world.

In the 1860s, Egypt was building the Suez Canal in partnership with France, while racking up a mountain of debt to European banks. Ultimately, the only way Egypt could discharge the debt was by selling its share of the Suez Canal to Great Britain. (Here is a lesson for nations that pile up debts that can never be repaid.) This arrangement gave Britain controlling seats in the Egyptian cabinet, and Egypt became a de facto protectorate of the British Empire. In 1922, the government of the United Kingdom issued a declaration of

Egyptian independence—but Egypt was not entirely free. The British government reserved four areas for itself: communications in Egypt, the defense of Egypt, the protection of foreigners and minorities in Egypt, and the administration of the Sudan. Though technically independent, Egypt remained under colonial domination.

That was the situation when Hasan al-Banna arrived on the scene in the 1920s. Strongly influenced by the radical Wahhabi Islamist movement in Saudi Arabia, al-Banna was determined to liberate Egypt from British rule and erase all non-Islamic influence. Al-Banna founded the Muslim Brotherhood in the ancient city of Ismailia, on the west bank of the Suez Canal. In March 1928, the Brotherhood consisted of just seven men: al-Banna and six men who worked for the Suez Canal Company.

He taught them that the only way to defeat the corrupting influence of the Christian West was to return to Sharia law, based on the Koran. A key requirement of Sharia law is an Islamic caliphate as the form of government. From this small beginning, the Muslim Brotherhood grew to an estimated two million members by the late 1940s.[16]

In 1939, Hasan al-Banna and the Brotherhood's inner circle formed a military wing called the Secret Apparatus. During World War II, the Brotherhood worked with Amin al-Husseini, the Grand Mufti of Jerusalem in British Mandate Palestine, engaging in agitation against the British, acts of terrorism, and recruiting Muslim soldiers to fight in the Nazi military during World War II. After the war, the

Brotherhood's Secret Apparatus carried out assassinations and acts of terror against Christians, Jews, and others in Egypt and against the fledgling nation of Israel. The goal of the Brotherhood was to achieve the formation of an Islamic state under Sharia law.[17]

In November 1948, Egyptian prime minister Mahmud Fahmi Nokrashi ordered a crackdown on the Muslim Brotherhood—so the Brotherhood assassinated Nokrashi in December 1948. In response, Egyptian government agents ambushed and killed Hasan al-Banna in Cairo in February 1949.

The founder was dead, but the Muslim Brotherhood lived on. In 1952, the Brotherhood supported a military coup that overthrew the Egyptian monarchy. The Brotherhood believed it had finally won a place of power in the Egyptian government—but the military junta that seized control had no intention of sharing power or lifting martial law in Egypt.

In October 1954, the Brotherhood attempted to assassinate the leader of the revolutionary junta, Colonel Gamal Abdel Nasser, as he gave a speech in Alexandria. A Brotherhood member, standing twenty-five feet from Nasser, fired eight shots—and all eight missed. The audience panicked, but Nasser appealed for calm. "My countrymen," he said, "I will live for your sake and die for the sake of your freedom and honor. Let them kill me; it does not concern me so long as I have instilled pride, honor, and freedom in you." Nasser's courage under fire sent his popularity soaring.[18]

The assassination attempt was a setback to the Muslim Brotherhood. Nasser rounded up the Brothers, executed some, and imprisoned the rest. The imprisoned Brotherhood members languished until Nasser died in 1971 and his successor, Anwar Sadat, released them.

After 1971, the Muslim Brotherhood began disguising its true aims, forming charitable front organizations to give the Brotherhood the appearance of a humanitarian agency. But the ultimate goal of the Muslim Brotherhood remains unchanged: undermining freedom and democracy while seeking to build a global Islamic state under Sharia law.

The Muslim Brotherhood has spread throughout the world, even forming chapters in major European capitals and across the United States. The logo of the Muslim Brotherhood consists of a green disk with two crossed swords and the command (in Arabic script), "Get Ready." This is a statement that the Brothers are to be always ready for *jihad*—the Arabic word for "struggle." (Jihad refers to the religious duty of Muslims to resist or struggle against those who do not follow Allah. As it is most frequently used, jihad has militaristic connotations. Read more about the concept of jihad in chapter 7.)

For many years the Muslim Brotherhood's publication in London, *Risalat al-Ikhwan* (Message of the Brotherhood), boldly declared on its front page, "Our Mission: World Domination."

In 2001, the Brotherhood removed the slogan—but its mission remains unchanged.

17

The Muslim Brotherhood's Strategy in America

During the Arab Spring uprisings, a reporter asked me, "Why should Americans care about what happens in Egypt, Syria, Libya, and the rest of the Arab world?"

My answer: our future is being written right now in the Arab world.

The Muslim Brotherhood and its fellow Islamists are bent on world domination. The Western mind-set cannot comprehend the militant Muslim mind-set, even though the Islamists have repeatedly told us that their intention is world domination. Our government, our media, our social institutions, and the Christian church are all in denial. When you suggest that these militant extremists are actively working to destroy our democracy and our Western way of life, people say, "Don't be so paranoid! America is too strong. That could never happen."

But consider this: Long before 9/11, Osama bin Laden had repeatedly declared war against America. The World Trade Center had already been bombed once in 1993. FBI counterterrorism specialist John O'Neill warned that Islamists would make another attempt on the World Trade Center, but his warnings went unheeded. (O'Neill himself died in the 9/11 attacks.)[19]

In the months leading up to 9/11, the FBI received repeated warnings from flight schools in California, Arizona, Minnesota, and Florida. The warnings stated that Middle Eastern men were taking lessons in how to fly Boeing passenger jets, yet they showed no interest in learning to take off or land. Just weeks before 9/11, the FBI received reports of planned hijackings of US airliners. The FBI even arrested al-Qaeda terrorist Zacarias Moussaoui at a flight school in St. Paul because he appeared to be planning to hijack a plane and crash it into the World Trade Center. That arrest came just days before 9/11.[20]

Why did America fail to heed the warnings that 9/11 was coming? Because, again, Americans cannot comprehend the militant Islamist mind-set. Our leaders could not imagine that anyone would ever hijack an airplane and fly it into a building, deliberately killing himself in order to inflict death and terror on America. And to a large degree, our leaders are still in denial today.

For years, Muslim journalists have been writing openly of the jihadist intentions of the Muslim Brotherhood and similar militant organizations. Our "politically correct" news organizations have become apologists for the Islamists.

In 2004, the FBI raided a suspected terrorist safe house in Annandale, Virginia, and discovered a secret basement containing a treasure trove of jihadist documents. One was called "An Explanatory Memorandum: On the General Strategic Goal for the Group in North America." That document, written by a top-level official of the Muslim Brotherhood and a senior Hamas leader, Mohammed Akram, was adopted by the Brotherhood's Shura Council and Organizational Conference in 1987. It contained this chilling mission statement:

The process of settlement [of Islamists in America] is a "Civilization-Jihadist Process" with all the word means. . . . The Ikhwan [the Arab name for the Brotherhood] must understand that their work in America is a kind of grand Jihad in eliminating and destroying the Western civilization from within, and "sabotaging" its miserable house by their hands and the hands of the believers, so that it is eliminated, and God's religion is made victorious over all other religions.[21]

The Muslim Brotherhood is pursuing a strategy of collapsing the United States from within, using our own political leaders and opinion leaders to advance the jihadist cause. Evidence of the success of these efforts came in February 2011, at the height of the Arab Spring uprisings, when President Obama's director of national intelligence, James Clapper, testified before the House Intelligence Committee. When Congresswoman Sue Myrick of North Carolina asked if the Muslim Brotherhood posed a threat to democracy in Egypt, Director Clapper said:

The term "Muslim Brotherhood" . . . is an umbrella term for a variety of movements, in the case of Egypt, a very heterogeneous group, largely secular, which has eschewed violence and has decried Al-Qaeda as a perversion of Islam. They have pursued social ends, a betterment of the political order in Egypt, et cetera. . . . In other countries, there are also chapters or franchises of the Muslim Brotherhood, but there is no overarching agenda, particularly in pursuit of violence, at least internationally.[22]

The notion that the Muslim Brotherhood is a "largely secular" group is bizarre. The name *Muslim* Brotherhood should be Mr. Clapper's first clue that the group is anything but secular. And how can the nation's director of national intelligence be unaware of the history of the organization and its overarching agenda of global domination by imposing Sharia law on the world? It is impossible to know why Mr. Clapper gave this testimony before a House committee, but we do know that what he said was utter nonsense.

Many people with Muslim Brotherhood ties have been appointed to influential positions in our government. For example, Rashad Hussain, the US special envoy to the Organization of the Islamic Conference (OIC), has given speeches at Brotherhood-affiliated events and has spoken in support of former University of South Florida professor Sami al-Arian, a Muslim Brotherhood member who pled guilty in 2006 to aiding the Palestine Islamic Jihad, a terrorist organization.[23]

Another example: Dalia Mogahed, of the President's Advisory Council on Faith-Based and Neighborhood Partnerships, has spoken in favor of Sharia law, saying that Muslim women *prefer* living under Sharia law because they associate it with "gender justice." Mogahed is also a vocal defender of two Muslim Brotherhood front groups, the Council on American-Islamic Relations (CAIR) and the

Islamic Society of North America (ISNA). In 2010, *Tablet* magazine called Dalia Mogahed "the most important person shaping the Obama Administration's Middle East message."[24]

President Obama also chose Ingrid Mattson, then-president of the Muslim Brotherhood front group ISNA, to offer an Islamic prayer at the National Cathedral as part of his first Inauguration Day ceremonies. Ingrid Mattson is a Canadian who was raised Catholic but left the Christian faith in her teens and converted to Islam in the 1980s. ISNA, the organization she headed in 2009, was named an unindicted co-conspirator in a plot to funnel millions of dollars to the terror group Hamas. Even so, President Obama sent his senior adviser, Valerie Jarrett, to give the keynote speech at the national convention of ISNA in 2009.[25]

Former FBI special agent John Guandolo states that the last three presidential administrations—Clinton, Bush, and Obama—have been penetrated to varying degrees by the Muslim Brotherhood. Guandolo adds that the Muslim Brotherhood has placed sympathizers and operatives in key positions in Homeland Security and the US military. All of this, he adds, is consistent with the Brotherhood's stated strategy of destroying Western civilization from within.[26]

Terrorism expert Walid Phares warns that American taxpayer dollars are helping to fund the Islamist agenda in the Middle East:

The Muslim Brotherhood . . . with Washington's stealthy backing . . . seized the revolution's microphone, positioned itself at the center of the uprising, and branded itself as the "soul" and "future" of the movement, even though the Muslim Brotherhood did not make up more than 15 percent of the mass of demonstrators. . . . Mr. Obama has sent billions in economic aid to a government controlled or significantly influenced by Islamists who . . . remain loyal to jihadi ideology.[27]

By funding the Islamists in Egypt and elsewhere in the Arab world, we are subsidizing jihad and the oppression of pro-democracy populations—and we are furthering their agenda of Islamic world domination!

We can see America's future in recent events in European nations, which have permitted a massive flow of Muslim immigrants into their borders. London, Paris, Amsterdam, Madrid, Brussels, Milan, Rome, and other European cities have been shaken by violent demonstrations and synagogue burnings by Islamist mobs. In London in 2010, the 2nd Battalion Royal Anglian Regiment arrived at London's Luton Airport after being deployed in Iraq. While most of the British citizens there waved flags of welcome for the returning heroes, a vocal group of Muslim protesters waved signs and shouted taunts of "Baby killers!" Some of the demonstrators later waved a banner declaring, "Islam will dominate the world. Freedom can go to hell!" and bragged to reporters that they were living on welfare, subsidized by British taxpayers, as they worked to subjugate British culture.[28]

In the West, and particularly in America, we prize the freedom to think for ourselves, to speak our minds, to choose our own religious and political affiliations, and to vote for the party and candidate of our choice. However, in the militant Muslim mind-set, the very freedoms we prize most are despised. Freedom, they say, can go to hell.

Is It Already Too Late?

Western civilization prizes ideals of intellectual enlightenment, liberty, tolerance, and peace. Militant Islamists demand conformity to an ancient and merciless code of laws. They have no concept of religious tolerance or religious freedom. Their worldview is stuck in the seventh century, and their way is not peace or compassion but jihad. Middle Eastern oil wealth and Western technologies have given these extremists enormous power to destabilize the world.

With a handful of box cutters, nineteen extremists brought war, death, and terror to the heart of America's two greatest cities on 9/11. They changed the direction of American foreign policy. Today, the American people are surrounded by surveillance cameras wherever they go. They submit to humiliating searches before boarding a commercial airplane. Since 2001, the global War on Terror has cost American taxpayers at least $4.4 trillion and has taken the lives of more than 6,800 US troops.[29]

After a dozen years of the War on Terror, you'd think the world would be safe for democracy. But as you look at Iraq, Afghanistan, and Pakistan—as you look around the Arab world—does it seem that freedom and democracy are winning? Or are we losing the global War on Terror, the war against Islamic extremism? The world is clearly becoming more dangerous, not less. America and the West are losing the war of ideas.

Is civilization on a downhill slope that leads inexorably to the Antichrist and Armageddon?

TWO

Ignored Warnings

MUCH OF THE ISLAMIC EXTREMISM and terrorism that afflicts our world today can be traced to one man whose name is virtually unknown in America: Sayyid Qutb.

Born in Egypt in 1906, Sayyid Qutb was a Sunni Muslim writer and intellectual. In 1949, he came to America and pursued studies at Colorado State Teachers College in Greeley, Colorado. His views on America and Western culture were profoundly shaped during that time. Greeley in the 1940s was a quiet town populated by moral and religious people, a dry town where alcohol was banned. Yet Qutb viewed Greeley (and by extension, all of America) as a cesspool of immorality, materialism, and injustice.

Many of Qutb's impressions were the result of simple culture shock. For example, he saw the lush green lawns in front of American homes as a symbol of greed and materialistic excess. It offended this son of the parched Egyptian desert to see gallons and gallons of water showered on lawns, and then to see Americans spending their weekends mowing and edging and manicuring those useless patches of grass.

He was rightly offended by segregation in America at that time, but he also expressed some weirdly twisted views on American history. For example, in his Arab-language article *"Amrika Allati Ra'itu"* (The America I Have Seen), he described the American Revolution as "a destructive war led by George Washington."[1] He was also offended by American support for the Jews and the newly founded State of Israel.

Why did Qutb view quiet little Greeley, Colorado, as such a cesspool of depravity and sin? I think the answer lies within Qutb himself. He was an introverted and socially isolated man who never married, claiming he could never find a woman of "sufficient moral purity and discretion."[2] In other words, he rationalized his awkwardness with the opposite sex as moral and spiritual superiority.

Every American woman he met seemed, to his distorted perception, like a wanton temptress. "The American girl," he wrote, "is well acquainted with her body's seductive capacity. She knows it lies in the face, and in expressive eyes, and thirsty lips. . . . She shows all this and does not hide it."[3] These sound like the words of a man who projects his own lusts onto other people because he doesn't dare acknowledge the sinful urges within himself.

His writings drip with loathing for American entertainment and culture. He saw American men as brutal and obsessed with sports. He wrote of "the spectacle of the fans as they follow a game of football . . . or watch boxing matches or bloody, monstrous wrestling matches." He called American churches "entertainment centers and sexual playgrounds."[4]

Immediately upon returning to Egypt, he joined the fundamentalist Muslim Brotherhood.

Qutb strongly rejected democracy and nationalism as Western ideas incompatible with Islam. He was the first Sunni Muslim to find a way around the ancient prohibition against overthrowing a Muslim ruler. His rationale: such rulers were no longer Muslims but infidels because they allowed Western modernization.

Sayyid Qutb's views on America are still influential in the Muslim world today. He has been called "the father of modern [Islamic] fundamentalism" and "the most famous personality of the Muslim world in the second half of the twentieth century."[5] His writings profoundly shaped the worldview of Islamic extremists such as Osama bin Laden and Ayman al-Zawahiri.

Qutb's description of American culture in the late 1940s is a bizarre caricature of the American reality. Yet we cannot deny that American culture has more than caught up with Qutb's caricature—and because the Hollywood version of America is the only America most Muslims have ever seen, Qutb's description of a corrupt, immoral, and violent America rings offensively true to the Islamic mind.[6]

The Slaughter of Innocents

After Colonel Gamal Abdel Nasser survived a botched assassination attempt by a Muslim Brotherhood member in 1954, the Egyptian revolutionary government rounded up thousands of Brothers. Most were imprisoned, and six ringleaders were tried and hanged.

One of those arrested was Sayyid Qutb, who was accused of being part of the Muslim Brotherhood's Secret Apparatus. In *The Looming Tower*, Lawrence Wright pointed out an unintended result of Sayyid Qutb's imprisonment:

> Stories about Sayyid Qutb's suffering in prison have formed a kind of Passion play for Islamic fundamentalists. It is said that Qutb had a high fever when he was arrested; nonetheless, the state-security officers handcuffed him and forced him to walk to prison. He fainted several times along the way. For hours he was held in a cell with vicious dogs, and then, during long periods of interrogation, he was beaten. . . .
>
> Three highly partisan judges, one of them Anwar al-Sadat, oversaw these proceedings. They sentenced Qutb to life in prison, but when his health deteriorated, the sentence was reduced to fifteen years.[7]

While in prison, Wright said, Qutb wrote his militant manifesto called *Ma'alim fi al-Tariq* (*Milestones*) and smuggled it out with the help of family and friends. For years, Qutb's writings were mimeographed and circulated, becoming underground classics. Finally, in 1964, the pieces of Qutb's manifesto were edited together and published in book form. The Egyptian government banned the book but could not suppress it.

In his writings, Sayyid Qutb divided the world into two parts: Islam and *jahiliyya* (pre-Islamic ignorance). According to Qutb, before the Prophet Muhammad delivered his divine message, the entire world was steeped in jahiliyya. Muslims, Qutb said, must reject all aspects of modern, non-Islamic culture, art, literature, law, government, science, and reason. He called Muslims to return to pure, primitive, seventh-century Islam.

"We need to initiate the movement of Islamic revival in some country," Qutb wrote. "There should be a vanguard which sets out with this determination and then keeps walking the path. I have written *Milestones* for this vanguard, which I consider to be a waiting reality about to be materialized."[8] Young Muslims read those revolutionary words and believed they heard the voice of Allah calling them to play a decisive role in history.

Qutb was released from prison and immediately began rebuilding the Secret Apparatus of the Muslim Brotherhood. Only six months after his release, he was arrested once more and charged with plotting to overthrow the government. During his three-month trial, he defiantly declared, "The time has come for a Muslim to give his head in order to proclaim the birth of the Islamic movement." He was convicted and sentenced to death. In response, Qutb thanked Allah and told the court, "I performed jihad for fifteen years until I earned this martyrdom."[9]

Sayyid Qutb was executed by hanging on August 29, 1966, yet his influence remains so strong that his ideology of armed jihad has become known as Qutbism (or Qutbiyya), a radical fundamentalist form of Sunni Islamist ideology.

Today, Sayyid Qutb is a hero and a martyr to Islamic fundamentalists, and his writings are studied across the Muslim world, from Morocco to Malaysia. It would not be an exaggeration to say that the 9/11 attacks had their genesis in Sayyid Qutb's strange American odyssey in Greeley, Colorado.

One of Qutb's most influential ideas is his interpretation of *takfir*, the Islamic principle of excommunication. Qutb. came to the conclusion that any Muslim who did not live out a radical, militant interpretation of Islam and the Koran was not a genuine Muslim. Takfir gave Qutb a rationale for ignoring the ancient prohibition against overthrowing a Muslim ruler. If a ruler didn't measure up to Qutb's high standards of Islamic perfection, then that ruler was no longer a true Muslim but an infidel. This gave Qutb the right to kill any Muslim who fell short of his standards of Islamic purity—including a ruler.[10]

This interpretation of takfir explains why Osama bin Laden came to the conclusion that the Islamic government of Saudi Arabia was illegitimate. He reasoned that, because the Saudis allowed American troops to walk on sacred Arabian soil, they were no longer true Muslims. Takfir also explains why Islamic terrorists like bin Laden and Zawahiri have killed far more Muslims than Christians or Jews.

For example, on November 19, 1995, Ayman al-Zawahiri carried out a massive car bomb attack against the Egyptian embassy in Islamabad, Pakistan. Sixteen innocent people died in the blast, plus two al-Qaeda suicide bombers. Sixty were injured. It was Zawahiri's first successful terror attack, and all of the victims were Muslims. The deaths of so many innocent Muslims alienated some of Zawahiri's followers, but he offered a Qutbist rationalization, as Lawrence Wright explains:

> [Zawahiri] explained that there were no innocents inside the embassy. Everyone who worked there, from the diplomats to the guards, was a supporter of the Egyptian regime, which had detained thousands of fundamentalists and blocked the rule of Islam. Those who carry out the duties of the government must shoulder responsibility for its crimes. No true Muslim could work for such a regime. In this, Zawahiri was repeating the takfir view. . . . Yes, he admitted, there might have been innocent victims—children, true believers—who also died, but Muslims are weak and their enemy is so powerful; in such an emergency, the rules against the slaughter of innocents must be relaxed.[11]

Zawahiri was also implicated in the successful plot to assassinate Egyptian president Anwar Sadat in 1981—a significant act of Qutbist takfir.

The Warning from Osama bin Laden

Osama bin Laden, a wealthy young Saudi, got his start in the jihadist struggle after the Soviet Union invaded Afghanistan in 1979. He was a scion of the bin Laden family, owners of the Saudi Binladin Group, a multinational oil, construction, and equity management conglomerate with reported earnings of $5 billion annually. Osama bin Laden used his own wealth—and raised millions from other wealthy Arabs—to fund the Afghan *mujahideen* insurgents in their struggle against the Soviet occupation. (The term *mujahideen* means "those engaged in jihad.") The United States also contributed money, weapons, and intelligence to aid the mujahideen against the Soviets.

Osama bin Laden operated a mujahideen training camp in Peshawar, Pakistan, called Maktab al-Khidamat. At the same time, Ayman al-Zawahiri worked as a physician at a Kuwaiti-financed Red Crescent hospital in Peshawar. The hospital was staffed and operated largely by the Muslim Brotherhood.[12]

When bin Laden came to al-Zawahiri's hospital to lecture, the two men formed a friendship and an alliance. Bin Laden was a wealthy, charismatic, devout idealist; Zawahiri was a propagandist and political strategist.

On August 11, 1988, bin Laden met with a number of senior leaders of a group called Egyptian Islamic Jihad. Much of the discussion revolved around the notion of transforming Egypt into a fundamentalist Islamic state. But the most momentous decision that came from that meeting was a vote to form a new organization to focus on global jihad: al-Qaeda (The Base).[13]

In February 1989, the Soviets left Afghanistan in defeat. Osama bin Laden returned to his hometown of Jeddah, Saudi

Arabia, as a conquering hero. Only thirty-one years old, he believed he had toppled the Soviet superpower. He gave no credit to American aid and the American-supplied Stinger missiles that knocked scores of Soviet planes and helicopters out of the air. He was convinced it was time to take on the next superpower—America.[14]

When Saddam Hussein launched the Iraqi invasion of Kuwait on August 2, 1990, the Saudi royal family feared that Saudi Arabia might be Iraq's next target. Brimming with self-confidence, Osama bin Laden met with Prince Sultan bin Abdulaziz al-Saud, the Saudi defense minister, and told him not to rely on the American unbelievers for defense. Instead, bin Laden urged al-Saud to let him and his army of mujahideen followers defend the border. The prince pointed out that the Iraqis had four thousand tanks, plus missiles and chemical weapons. How did bin Laden propose to fight Saddam Hussein?

"We fight him with faith," bin Laden replied.[15]

The Saudis refused bin Laden's offer and turned to the United States for help. The presence of American troops on Saudi soil enraged bin Laden. He denounced the "unjust American occupation of the land of the two mosques" (Mecca and Medina) and denounced the Saudis for profaning the sacred soil of Arabia.[16] From then on, bin Laden aimed his terror plots at the West, especially the United States.

In August 1996, bin Laden issued a *fatwa*, or Islamic religious edict, against the United States. Published in *Al-Quds Al Arabi*, a London-based Arabic newspaper, the fatwa was called "Declaration of War against the Americans Occupying the Land of the Two Holy Places." It was a declaration of jihad to expel American troops from Islamic lands.[17] In February 1998, bin Laden and Zawahiri issued another fatwa calling on Muslims to "kill the Americans and plunder their money wherever and whenever they find it." They also said that the slaughter of Americans and their allies was "an individual duty for every Muslim."[18]

"Bin Laden declared war on us," former New York City mayor Rudy Giuliani said on NBC's *Meet the Press*. "We didn't hear it. I thought it was pretty clear at the time, but a lot of people couldn't see it."[19] So we were caught napping when 9/11 exploded on our collective consciousness. Osama bin Laden warned us, but we didn't listen.

Why Do They Hate Us?

An extreme sect of Islam has declared war on Western civilization, on the United States of America, and on Christians and Jews. While the War on Terror is not a religious war— that is, it's not a war of one religion versus another—it's clear that militant, extremist Islam has declared war on us. To pretend otherwise is to be in denial.

Again and again, America has taken up the cause of oppressed Muslim people. In the 1980s, America helped the Muslim mujahideen defend themselves against the Soviet occupation of Afghanistan. In the early 1990s, America defended Muslim Bosnians against genocidal attacks by Serbs in the former Yugoslavia. In the late 1990s, America defended Muslim

Kosovo Albanians against Serb-instigated genocide in Kosovo. When America stationed troops in Saudi Arabia during the first Gulf War, we did so to prevent Muslims from killing Muslims. America liberated Muslim Kuwait and Muslim Iraq from the tyrannical regime of Saddam Hussein. Most recently, America and its NATO allies helped liberate Muslim Libya from the tyranny of Colonel Muammar Gaddafi.

In spite of all the blood and money America has sacrificed to defend Muslims around the world, Muslim extremists still want to do us harm. The extremists don't just hate our government. They hate *us*. Osama bin Laden and Ayman al-Zawahiri issued fatwas ordering Muslims to kill *all* Americans and *all* American allies, wherever they might be found.

Radical Islamists hate the West for a variety of reasons. They remember how Western nations colonized and exploited the Arab world. They hate the immorality and blasphemy they see in our entertainment media. They believe America's economic success is the result of greed and exploitation. They hate America's support for Israel. They despise Americans for being (in their minds) weak, soft, and decadent.

The religious divide between the West and the Muslim world should not be underestimated—even though many of the Islamists' views of America and Western culture are wildly distorted. Osama bin Laden's statements about America are saturated with religious imagery and theological language. In May 1998, two months before the US embassy bombings in Kenya and Tanzania, bin Laden told ABC News reporter John Miller:

The call to wage war against America was made because America has spear-headed the crusade against the Islamic nation, sending tens of thousands of its troops to the land of the two Holy Mosques over and above its meddling in its affairs and its politics, and its support of the oppressive, corrupt and tyrannical regime that is in control. These are the reasons behind the singling out of America as a target.[20]

Osama bin Laden's carefully chosen word *crusade* is an explicitly religious term. It demonstrates his twisted view that America today is carrying on the tradition of the Crusades—a series of wars for control of the Holy Land in the eleventh through thirteenth centuries, long before Columbus discovered America. The belief that America is waging a theocratic "crusade against the Islamic nation" would be laughable if it weren't such a dangerous notion.

When bin Laden speaks of "the Islamic nation," he does not mean one specific political entity, such as Iraq or Saudi Arabia. All the nations and peoples of the Muslim world comprise the so-called Islamic nation. Muslims see the boundaries between nations as territorial divisions imposed by Western colonial mapmakers. Once the entire world is united under Sharia law and Islamic religion, there will only be one nation—the Islamic global Caliphate—united under one leader, a coming Islamic savior who will be known as the *Mahdi*. (Find more on the Mahdi in chapter 5.)

To bin Laden and his fellow Muslim fundamentalists, the war against Western civilization has always been a war of Islam versus unbelief. As bin Laden went on to say:

> Our call is the call of Islam that was revealed to Mohammad. It is a call to all mankind. We have been entrusted with good cause to follow in the footsteps of the Messenger [Mohammad] and to communicate his message to all nations. It is an invitation that we extend to all the nations to embrace Islam, the religion that calls for justice, mercy and fraternity among all nations. . . . We are entrusted to spread this message and to extend that call to all the people. We, nonetheless, fight against their governments and all those who approve of the injustice they practice against us. We fight the governments that are bent on attacking our religion and on stealing our wealth and on hurting our feelings.[21]

Bin Laden also stated that al-Qaeda's acts of terrorism were "of the commendable kind" that were "directed at the tyrants and the aggressors and the enemies of Allah. . . . Tyrants and oppressors who subject the Arab nation to aggression ought to be punished."[22] We have to wonder how many actual "tyrants and oppressors" of Muslims died in the World Trade Center and the Pentagon and United Airlines Flight 93 on 9/11. The ability of the radical Islamists to rationalize the slaughter of innocent people as a holy service to Allah is beyond the comprehension of Western minds.

Other Voices from the Islamic World

Queen Rania al-Abdullah of Jordan appeared on the Oprah Winfrey program on October 5, 2001, less than a month after 9/11. Oprah asked her, "When this first happened on September 11, I think it came as a shock to so many of us that other people in the world hated us so much. Can you help explain that to us?" The then-thirty-one-year-old Queen of Jordan responded:

> I think it's very important that you realize that for the majority of Muslims, they do not hate Americans. They do not hate the American way of life. In fact, many countries look at the American model as one that needs to be replicated, one that they aspire to achieve.
>
> We are talking about a minority of people who feel that they have been unjustly treated by the United States. Some of them feel that US foreign policy might have been partial and not completely fair to all parties involved, and they wanted their voice to be heard. Unfortunately, the means that they have used are ones that are condemned all over the Arab world.[23]

It's true that terrorist acts are perpetrated by an extremist minority within the Muslim community—but where is the voice of the majority? Where is the condemnation of terrorism that we should hear from the mainstream Muslim community? Are moderates afraid to speak up and condemn the extremists in their midst? Are they afraid of what Islamic extremists will do to them or their families if they speak out? Whatever the reason, Muslim condemnation of terrorism has been muted.

In May 2014, Pew Research Center released the findings of its polling across eleven Muslim countries, and stated that support for al-Qaeda is "low" across the Muslim world. How did Pew define "low" support for al-Qaeda? Pew stated that "a median of only 13 percent . . . had a favorable view of al-Qaeda, while 57 percent had an unfavorable opinion of the terrorist group." The Pew report also noted that "substantial minorities of Muslims in Lebanon (33 percent) and Egypt (25 percent) said that suicide bombing is an acceptable tactic in defense of Islam. And in the Palestinian territories, 62 percent of Muslims said this."[24]

It's a matter of opinion whether those numbers reflect "low" support for terrorism in the Islamic community. To me, the fact that only a little more than half of the Muslim community has an "unfavorable" opinion of the most notorious terrorist group in history is troubling. And the fact that 13 percent of the world's 1.6 billion Muslims have a "favorable" opinion of al-Qaeda means there are roughly 208 million pro-al-Qaeda Muslims in the world. So we have to ask: is it accurate to characterize that as "low" support for al-Qaeda?

The Indoctrination of American Muslims

Even in mainstream Muslim communities, young Muslim-Americans are being indoctrinated in some very un-American ways of thinking. A month after the 9/11 attacks, *Washington Post* reporter Marc Fisher talked to young American-born Muslims, all US citizens, at the Muslim Community School in Potomac. They had no conception of how rare it is in this world to enjoy American-style freedoms, no conception of how blessed they were to live under the protection of the Bill of Rights.

One Muslim seventh-grader named Miriam shrugged off the specialness of being an American citizen, asking, "What does it really mean to be an American? Being American is just being born in this country." Ibrahim, an eighth-grader, added, "Being an American means nothing to me. I'm not even proud of telling my cousins in Pakistan that I'm American." An eleventh-grader named Kamal, however, said, "I love being an American," though he wondered if "maybe we might have done things to [the terrorists'] country that weren't right," and that led to the 9/11 attacks.[25]

When the *Post* reporter asked the principal of the Muslim school if he thought that Osama bin Laden was responsible for 9/11, the principal changed the subject to Israel. "I don't know Osama bin Laden," he said. "But whatever is said about him, I want it said about the Israeli prime minister. If we're going after terrorism, let's go at it at the roots, not the branches."[26]

These were common responses from the Muslim community after 9/11. Muslims often denied or expressed skepticism that Muslims were involved. Or they suggested that American foreign policy was to blame for 9/11. Or they drew a moral equivalence between Israel and al-Qaeda.

Around the world, many Muslims cheered the hijackers as heroes and martyrs in the cause of Islam. In Egypt, university students burned US and Israeli flags and chanted, "Arrogant George Bush, tomorrow you will reap the fruits of your war!"[27] In Indonesia, hundreds of Islamic activists clashed with police outside the US Embassy in Jakarta. In the Philippines, five thousand Muslim protesters chanted "Death to America!" and "Long live Osama bin Laden!" as they burned American flags. In the Gaza Strip, two Palestinians were killed and seventy-six injured in protests against America.[28]

The response from the Arab world is reminiscent of the rhetoric heard during the Iranian Revolution of 1979. As described in chapter 1, after Iranian revolutionaries took fifty-two Americans hostage in Tehran, the Ayatollah Khomeini declared, "The governments of the world should know that Islam cannot be defeated. Islam will be victorious in all the countries of the world, and Islam and all the teachings of the Koran will prevail all over the world."[29]

Khomeini was not expressing a distorted view of Islam. The global supremacy of the Koran is basic Islamic doctrine. Though his words made little sense to Westerners, his statements made perfect sense to the Muslim world. The goal of every serious Muslim is to see that the teachings of the Koran prevail across the world.

The Rise of Militant Islam

Islam is spreading faster today than at any other time in history, and it currently boasts about 1.6 billion adherents. Roughly one out of five people in the world is Muslim. Islam reigns as the dominant religion in forty-five nations. The spread of Islam as a whole has encouraged the rise of militant Islam—and militant Islam is the original and authentic Islam of the seventh century.

We can no longer afford to be ignorant. The 9/11 attacks took away our innocence about the world. We must open our eyes and see that the real cause of terrorism is hate. Militant Islamists hate all that Christians believe, stand for, hope for, and love. They hate our freedom. They hate our message of Christlike love, which they see as weakness. They hate our Christian gospel, which they see as blasphemy. The notion of a tolerant society that guarantees religious liberty is foreign to them. Their mission is to bring the entire world under submission to the Koran and Sharia law.

It's not enough to defeat militant Islam on the battlefield. The War on Terror is ultimately a battle for the human mind and heart. We are engaged in a struggle of eternal significance.

We must open our eyes to understand this enemy—and to recognize the weapons and the strategy God has given us for the battle.

THREE

The Prophet
and the Koran

A NUMBER OF YEARS AGO, a militant Muslim said to me, "You Christians are all cowards!"

"Why do you say that?" I asked.

"You claim to believe in Jesus," he said, "but you never defend him. The name of Jesus is used as a curse word in your American movies and TV shows. Movie people don't dare to speak blasphemy against the Prophet Muhammad, because they know that Muslims would kill them for it. But Hollywood doesn't fear Christians. If you Christians weren't such cowards, you would rise up and kill every actor and movie producer who blasphemes your Jesus."

This young Muslim put his finger on a major difference between Christianity and Islam. In Christianity, God has promised to avenge attacks against His people. We trust the One who said, "Vengeance is mine; I will repay" (Romans 12:19 KJV)—but to the Muslim mind, this makes us look like cowards. In Islam, it's the opposite: the people are commanded to punish insults to the honor of Allah and Muhammad.

Who was this man Muhammad, who died almost fourteen centuries ago but who is still the object of such zeal and devotion?

A Vision in a Cave

Born in Mecca in the autumn of AD 570, Muhammad received his name from his mother and grandfather. It was a rare name among ancient Arabs, and it meant "highly praised." His father, a trader named Abdullah, died before Muhammad was born. Muhammad spent most of his childhood years with his nurse, Halima, among the Beni Saad tribesmen.

As a child, Muhammad returned to his mother's home in Mecca, but she became ill and died. He was cared for by his grandfather, who soon died, and then by his uncle, Abu Talib. When Muhammad was twelve, he went with his uncle on a business trip to Syria. The journey took several months and exposed young Muhammad to many new ideas and experiences. He and his uncle visited Jewish settlements in Palestine and Christian communities in Syria.

As a young man in Mecca, Muhammad was influenced by Jewish and Christian teachers and preachers who expounded on their faith at the annual fairs in the city. Though Muhammad could not read, he listened intently to these recitations and sermons, and he absorbed a smattering of information (and misinformation) about Judaism and Christianity.

Little else is known about Muhammad's early years. Like other young men, he probably tended sheep and goats in the neighboring hills and valleys. Authorities agree that he was respected for his serious and thoughtful nature, and for his personal integrity. He was nicknamed al-Amin, "the trustworthy one."

At age twenty-five, Muhammad again traveled to Syria. This time, he delved into the practices and beliefs of the Syrian Christians. Later, as he dictated the writings of the Koran, he spoke of Christians with respect. He had no sympathy for their doctrine, however, and little understanding of the teachings of Jesus.

Muhammad had two major objections to the Christian gospel, as it was presented to him by the Syrian Christians. One was the role of Mary; the other was the divinity of Jesus. According to Sir William Muir, the gospel that Muhammad heard was tragically distorted:

Instead of the simple majesty of the Gospel—as a revelation of God reconciling mankind to Himself through His Son—the sacred dogma of the Trinity was forced upon the traveler with . . . misleading and offensive zeal . . . and the worship of Mary [was] exhibited in so gross a form as to leave the impression upon the mind of Mahomet [Muhammad] that she was held to be a goddess, if not the third Person [of the Trinity] and consort of the Deity.[1]

The Arab pagans believed the gods could have sexual intercourse with human women, thereby producing children called "the sons of the gods." Muhammad rejected the idea that God could father a child through a human woman. Christians believe Mary conceived Jesus, the Son of God, not as a result of sexual intercourse (as in pagan myths) but as a miraculous work of the Holy Spirit. Because Muhammad misunderstood the virgin birth, he rejected the belief that Jesus was born of God and refused to call Jesus "the Son of God." Instead, he called Jesus "the son of Mary."

Upon his return from Syria, Muhammad married a woman named Khadija, who was fifteen years older than Muhammad and had been married twice before. She remained Muhammad's only wife as long as she lived. After her death, Muhammad took nine other wives and more concubines.

Nearing age forty, Muhammad pondered the question, "What is truth?" He was also troubled by the social injustice he saw among the clans in his tribe. Muhammad's Hashemite clan was the poorer of two main clans in the Quraysh tribe. He wanted to create a more equitable social system to protect the poor, the widows, and the orphans.

Muhammad frequently went alone into the hills near Mecca to meditate. His favorite place was a cave about two or three miles north of the city. According to the account of Ibn Ishaq, the first biographer of Muhammad, the future prophet was sound asleep when the angel Gabriel appeared and commanded, "Recite!"

Startled and afraid, Muhammad asked, "What shall I recite?"
He felt his throat tighten as if the angel were choking him.

"Recite!" the angel commanded again.

Yet the angel continued to choke him.

"Recite!" the angel said a third time. "Recite in the name
of the Lord, the Creator who created man from a clot of
blood! Recite! Your Lord is most gracious. It is he who has
taught man by the pen that which he does not know."

From that day forward, Muhammad preached the message
of "Allah"—his name for the Creator. The first section of the
Koran has a title that literally means "recitation." Muhammad's
own account of his revelation is worth noting:

> Inspiration cometh in one of two ways; sometimes
> Gabriel communicateth the Revelation to me, as one
> man to another, and this is easy; at other times, it is like
> the ringing of a bell, penetrating my very heart, and
> rending me; and this it is which afflicteth me the most.[2]

Muhammad returned from this experience in the cave and
told his wife, Khadija, that God had commissioned him to
preach. She consulted with her *hanif* kinsman (a hanif is a holy
man who holds to the pure monotheistic beliefs of the patri-
arch Ibrahim, or Abraham). The hanif listened to the story and
then declared that Muhammad had been chosen, like Moses,
to receive divine inspiration and to be the prophet of his people. As long as Khadija lived, she gave unfailing support to
Muhammad, though many in Mecca rejected his message.

The people of Mecca initially scoffed at Muhammad because he was illiterate. But Muhammad used his inability to read to his advantage by stating that his illiteracy substantiated his claim to have received his revelations directly from Allah. Down through the centuries, Muslims have regarded Muhammad's vision as sacred and his recitation as a miraculous act of God, though Muhammad himself did not work any miracles. Muhammad stressed his ordinary humanity as a prophet. As a result, Muslims take pride in the fact that they do not call themselves Muhammadans, because such a term would imply that they worship Muhammad as Christians worship Christ.

After receiving his initial revelation, Muhammad became depressed when he received no further messages from God. He even contemplated suicide during this period because he felt uncertain about himself and his mission.

Muhammad Emerges from Obscurity

Around age forty-four, Muhammad emerged from his doubts and his obscurity. He asserted unequivocally that Allah had ordained him as a prophet and had commissioned him to go to the people of Arabia. He recited warnings, exhortations, and messages as coming directly from Allah. He taught that Allah was the one God and that men must thank him for their existence and worship him only. He preached equality and justice before God, and he warned that a Day of Judgment was coming for all men.

Muhammad's wife, Khadija, was his first convert, followed by his slave Zaid, whom he later adopted as a son.

Then he converted two of his most trusted friends, Abu Bakr and Umar, who later succeeded him as leaders of the Muslim movement.

In Mecca, however, Muhammad encountered harsh opposition from his own tribe. His people refused to acknowledge him as a prophet and refused to give up idol worship.

The Jews in the area, however, did not oppose Muhammad as much as his own tribesmen did. So Muhammad developed a close relationship with the Jews, some of whom acknowledged him as a prophet, others as the Messiah descended from Abraham. The majority of Jews took a "wait and see" attitude. Muhammad incorporated many Jewish traditions and stories into his new religion, though it's not clear whether he was influenced by those stories—or simply included them to gain favor with the Jews.

The Koran includes the stories of Abraham and Ishmael, Hagar and Ishmael, Joseph and Jacob, and the account of the destruction of Sodom and Gomorrah. In the Koran, these stories are usually mixed with other stories, myths, and legends that come from extrabiblical sources.

Muhammad's unsuccessful attempt to win the hearts of the people of Mecca was deeply frustrating to him. In his discouragement, Muhammad and his followers moved to the city of Medina in a mass migration known as the *hijra*. In Medina, Muhammad struck a more responsive chord in the people's hearts. The city had a large community of Jews; in fact, three of the five tribes living in the city were Jewish. The Jews of Medina had often warned the Arab tribes in the area that the coming Messiah would punish them for their wickedness and injustices. Unlike the more worldly people of Mecca, the people of Medina were ripe for Muhammad's message of a new monotheistic religion.

In Medina, Muhammad brought Jews and pagans together under the banner of Allah. He managed to please the Jews by adopting some of their religious rites. The Jewish Day of Atonement became the Muslim fast day of Ashura. Prayer was increased from two to three times daily to accommodate the Jewish morning, midday, and evening prayers—then later increased to five times daily. Muslims held a public service, such as the Jews had in their synagogues. The Muslims declared Friday to be their holy day, an accommodation to the Jewish Sabbath, which began at sundown on Friday. Muhammad even adopted the Jewish call to prayer, but instead of using the trumpet of the Jews, he chose to use a human prayer caller, or *muezzin*, who would issue the call to prayer from the minaret of a mosque.

Later, when the Jews began to reject Muhammad's message, he became angry and accused the Jews of rejecting the truth. He claimed Jewish property as his own. By the time he left Medina, Muslim Arabs controlled the city, and the two Arab tribes that had lost virtually everything to the Jews were restored to power and prestige.

Muhammad and Christians

Muhammad never showed an interest in courting Christians to his cause or in adopting Christian rituals and beliefs, yet he was not hostile toward Christians. In fact, he had a generally favorable attitude toward Christian people, though he strongly disagreed with the tenets of their faith.

Tradition holds that shortly after Muhammad's initial revelation, Khadija's cousin, Waraqa ibn Naufal, translated portions of the New Testament into Hebrew and Arabic. Waraqa tutored Muhammad in the Christian faith, but he died soon after beginning his mentoring relationship with Muhammad. Some attribute Muhammad's "confused period" (which occurred soon after his initial revelation) to an intense personal struggle with the Christian ideas Waraqa tried to teach him.

The Progression of Muhammad's Teachings

There was a step-by-step progression to Muhammad's teachings. At each stage he became increasingly more extreme and grandiose.

First, Muhammad sought to warn and reform the pagan society of the Arabian Peninsula. He felt a burden to call people to turn to the one true God, the God of Abraham.

Next, he equated his revelation with that of Judaism and Christianity, perceiving himself to be on an equal footing with Moses and Jesus (Isa).

Finally, Muhammad saw himself and his message as the final word of God that superseded both Judaism and Christianity. He was convinced that, because the Jews and Christians had moved away from God's intended purposes, God had sent him to proclaim the ultimate revelation. He claimed that his teachings rose triumphant over both the Jewish Law and the Christian gospel.

In the end, Muhammad claimed that Islam was the universal faith—a faith that had started with Abraham (whom Muhammad called the first Muslim). At the same time, Muhammad was strict in his belief that the new message of Allah was announced in the Arabic language and intended for Arabs, who henceforth would have a prophet and a holy book of their own.

To Muhammad, the Jew was to follow the Law and the Christian was to hold fast to the gospel. Both Jews and Christians were to admit the apostleship of Muhammad and the authority of the Koran as being equal to their own respective prophets, teachers, and writings. As the Koran states: "Say: 'O People of the Book! ye have no ground to stand upon unless ye stand fast by the Law, the Gospel, and all the revelation that has come to you from your Lord'" (Koran 5:68).

At first, the Jews living on the Arabian Peninsula saw Muhammad as their ally. This alliance between Muhammad and the Arabian Jews lasted as long as Muhammad saw his mission as a protest against error and superstition, because the Jews also opposed error and superstition.

But as Islam became more exclusive and demanded to have priority over other religions, the Jews backed away. By the time Muhammad began his farewell pilgrimage, he had barred Christians and Jews from visiting the Kaaba. (The Kaaba, the cube-shaped "house of Allah" in Mecca, is the central shrine of the Islamic religion. According to Islam, the Kaaba was built by Abraham and his son Ishmael, and it is located near the Well of Zamzam, which Muslims claim is the well that sustained Ishmael and his mother Hagar when they wandered in the desert.) Muhammad claimed it was a divine command that non-Muslims be excluded from this holy site until they confessed the supremacy of Islam or consented to pay tribute.

Muhammad initially used the ancient legend about Abraham and Ishmael to legitimize his new religion. He argued that Islam's relationship to Abraham made Islam the equal of Judaism and Christianity. Later in life, however, Muhammad revised this claim, stating that his revelation superseded both Judaism and Christianity and had become the final revelation of God.

The Koran: The Supreme Book of Islam

Muslims believe that God has spoken to the human race throughout the ages, and specifically through people called prophets. Muslims regard Muhammad as the final prophet of God. Islam acknowledges other prophets before Muhammad's time, including the great figures of the Old and New Testaments such as Abraham, Moses, David, and Jesus. But Islam contends that God gave Muhammad the complete revelation of the final divine truth.

This ultimate knowledge of God, they say, is found only in the pages of the Koran, the collection of Muhammad's proclamations that his followers memorized and recorded. It is through Muhammad that Allah allegedly made known the fullness of his laws and spelled out precisely what he expects from man, morally, ethically, and religiously.

Muslims believe that the Koran is explicit and literal, and human beings must obey the Koran literally in order to comply with God's rules. Islamic extremists and fundamentalists complain that the Koran has been interpreted figuratively by nonpurists, and that any nonliteral interpretation of the Koran is a compromise with Western godlessness.

Islam holds that all mankind should submit to Allah's will, as revealed in the Koran. The enforcement of Islamic law—which Muslims view as God's law on earth—is of paramount importance to zealous Muslims. The enforcement of the Koran is at the root of all Islamic fundamentalist regimes, such as the Islamic Republic of Iran and Saudi Arabia. The zeal to enforce the decrees of the Koran is what drives the radical fundamentalism of the Taliban and similar fanatical groups. Those who attain the power to impose Islamic law on society usually do so without mercy.

The Ayatollah Khomeini, for example, did not spare the lives of his closest friends and allies whom he suspected of disloyalty to the Islamic government of Iran. One historian writes:

Khomeini believed that spies and traitors were everywhere. In his zeal to root out enemies, Khomeini turned on his own loyal followers. In a series of spectacular trials, inner members of Khomeini's own circle gave forced confessions on national television.

They confessed to spying and plotting to overthrow the Islamic government.[3]

Are there moderate Muslims? If by "moderate" we mean less zealous and less extreme, then there are certainly moderate Muslims. Yet these moderate Muslims have good reason to be fearful when extremist Muslims take political control of a nation. Much of the freedom that moderate Muslims enjoy, including the freedom to interpret the Koran according to their own conscience, vanishes under fundamentalist Islamic rule. And one reason moderate Muslims do not speak out against the excesses of the fundamentalists is that they know the fundamentalists do not hesitate to respond with force and cruelty.

The Koran is composed of 114 *suras* (chapters), but they are not arranged in any historical, chronological, or thematic order. As a result, it is impossible to determine at what stage in Muhammad's life these "revelations" came to him, and many of these "revelations" contradict each other. The suras are arranged in order of length, beginning with the longest and progressing toward the shortest.

Muhammad, being illiterate, did not write down these revelations. He spoke his revelations and then his followers acted as scribes, writing his revelations on any available paperlike material, from leaves to dried bones to scraps of parchment.

Several Muslim scholars have tried to put events in the Koran into a chronological order. One scholar, Ibn-Ishaq, gives this order: Creation; Adam and Eve; Noah and his offspring; Hud; Salih; Abraham; Lot; Job; Shu'ayb; Joseph;

Moses; Ezekiel; Elijah; Elisha; Samuel; David; Solomon; Sheba; Isaiah; al-Khidr; Daniel; Hananiah; Azariah; Mishael and Ezra; Alexander; Zechariah and John (the Baptist); the family of Imran and Jesus, son of Mary; the Companion of the Cave; Jonah; the Three Messengers; Samson; and George of Lydda (whom Christians call "Saint George").[4]

As you read through this list, you notice that many of the so-called prophets from the Koran are not mentioned in either Old or New Testament texts. It is also apparent that many of the biblical characters listed are not in historical order. This is due to the fact that Muhammad had a sketchy knowledge of the Bible.

The Koran and the Bible

If you read the Koran, you soon find that it differs significantly from the Bible with regard to various events. Here are a few of the differences:

- In the Koran, one of Noah's sons separated himself from the rest of the family and died in the floodwaters. After the flood, the ark came to rest on Mount Judi in the Anatolian range of modern Turkey (Koran 11:32–48).

   In the Bible, all members of Noah's family were spared, and the ark came to rest on Mount Ararat in the Armenian highland of Turkey (Genesis 7:1–13; 8:4).

- In the Koran, Abraham dwelled in a "valley without cultivation" by the Kabah (Koran 14:37), a valley thought to have been the valley of Mecca.

  In the Bible, Abraham dwelled in Hebron, nineteen miles south of modern Jerusalem (Genesis 13:18).

- In the Koran, the wife of Pharaoh plucked Moses from the river, saying, "Slay him not. It may be that he will be of use to us" (Koran 28:9).

  In the Bible, the daughter of Pharaoh took Moses from the river, sparing his life out of compassion (Exodus 2).

- In the Koran, the first miracle assigned to Jesus is the making of a clay bird and then breathing life into it so it became a living bird (Koran 3:49).

  In the Bible, the first miracle of Jesus is turning water into wine at the marriage feast in Cana (John 2:1–11).

- In the Koran, Zechariah is speechless for three nights (Koran 3:38–41; 19:16–34).

  In the Bible, Zechariah is mute from the time the angel speaks to him until after John the Baptist is born (Luke 1).

- In the Koran, Jesus was not crucified; instead, it was only made to seem to the witnesses that he was crucified (Koran 4:157).

  In the Bible, Jesus was crucified, buried, and raised again (Matthew 17; Mark 15; Luke 23; John 19).

- The Koran says of Jesus: "Christ the son of Mary was no more than a messenger" (Koran 5:75).

  The Bible presents Jesus this way: "In the past God spoke to our ancestors through the prophets at many times and in various ways, but in these last days he has spoken to us by his Son, whom he appointed heir of all things, and through whom also he made the universe. The Son is the radiance of God's glory and the exact representation of his being, sustaining all things by his powerful word. After he had provided purification for sins, he sat down at the right hand of the Majesty in heaven" (Hebrews 1:1–3).

- The Koran says that "Allah loveth not those who reject Faith" and "Allah loveth not those who do wrong" (Koran 3:32, 57).

  The Bible says that "God so loved the world that he gave his one and only Son, that whoever believes in him shall not perish but have eternal life" (John 3:16) and "while we were still sinners, Christ died for us" (Romans 5:8).

- The Koran says to men that they are to be the "protectors and maintainers of women" but also tells men to "beat" their wives for disloyalty or bad behavior (Koran 4:34). Regarding sexual relations, the Koran tells husbands, "Your wives are as a tilth [a piece of farmland, a place of sowing seed] unto you; so approach your tilth when or how ye will" (Koran 2:223).

The Bible says, "Husbands, love your wives, just as Christ loved the church and gave himself up for her" (Ephesians 5:25) and "Husbands, in the same way be considerate as you live with your wives, and treat them with respect as the weaker partner and as heirs with you of the gracious gift of life" (1 Peter 3:7).

- The Koran says of our relationship to God: "(Both) the Jews and the Christians say: 'We are sons of Allah, and his beloved.' Say: 'Why then doth He punish you for your sins? Nay, ye are but men, of the men he hath created: He forgiveth whom He pleaseth, and He punisheth whom He pleaseth: and to Allah belongeth the dominion of the heavens and the earth, and all that is between: and unto Him is the final goal (of all)" (Koran 5:18).

The Bible says of our relationship to God: "We are children of God, and what we will be has not yet been made known. But we know that when Christ appears, we shall be like him, for we shall see him as he is" (1 John 3:2).

Do Muslims Read the Koran?

Few Muslims have actually read their own holy book. Reza F. Safa, a former radical Shiite Muslim who converted to Christianity, has written, "I have more knowledge of the Koran now as a Christian than I ever had as a fanatical Muslim. Of all the Muslims I knew, only a handful had some knowledge of the Koran. Even today when I confront many fanatical Muslims with strange revelations of Muhammad in the Koran, they are unaware these verses are in the book."[5] There are several reasons Muslims do not read the Koran.

First, illiteracy among Muslims is high. In some Muslim nations in Asia and Africa, 75 to 85 percent of the people cannot read or write.

Second, many Muslims are too poor to own a copy of the Koran. The book has not been widely published or circulated to the poor, in part because reading the Koran is not emphasized as a spiritual discipline. Knowledge of the Koran is not one of the Five Pillars of Islam that all Muslims are expected to observe (more on the Five Pillars in chapter 6).

Third, Muslims believe the Koran must be read in Arabic, which is spoken only by Arab Muslims. Translations in non-Arabic languages are not considered the genuine Koran but a mere interpretation of the Koran. Yet of the more than one billion people who call themselves Muslims, eight hundred million of them cannot read, write, or speak Arabic. Even those who can read Arabic rarely read the Koran. Many consider the language too poetic or difficult to understand.

If Muslims do not read the Koran, how do they know what the Koran teaches? They know only the interpretation of the Koran that has been given by their religious leaders.

The Hadith stands next to the Koran in the writings of Islam. It is a collection of Islamic traditions, including sayings and deeds of Muhammad as heard by his contemporaries or related in a second- or third-hand way. Many of the sayings are commentaries on the teachings of the Koran, and many Muslims are unable to differentiate the Hadith from the Koran.

The Koran's View of the Bible

There is little to be gained by arguing the accuracy of the Bible versus the Koran with Muslims. They are routinely taught in Islam that the Bible has been corrupted or altered. Many Muslims believe the Gospel accounts (Matthew, Mark, Luke, and John) have been edited and altered over the past two thousand years. For example, Muslims teach that when Jesus spoke of sending another Comforter to His followers after He left the earth, Jesus meant Muhammad, not the Holy Spirit.

Ironically, while modern-day Islam rejects the Gospel accounts as corrupt, the Koran itself commands Muslims to read the *Injeel*—that is, the Gospel accounts of the life of Jesus. Few Muslims are aware of this command, and they are equally unaware of these statements in the Koran about the Bible:

- "Say ye: 'We believe in Allah, and the revelation given to us, and to Abraham, Isma'il, Isaac, Jacob, and the Tribes, and that given to Moses and Jesus, and that given to (all) prophets from their Lord: We make no difference between one and another of them: And we bow to Allah (in Islam)'" (Koran 2:136).
- "If thou wert in doubt as to what We have revealed unto thee, then ask those who have been reading the Book [that is, the Bible] from before thee: the Truth

hath indeed come to thee from thy Lord: so be in no wise of those in doubt" (Koran 10:94).

- In the Koran, Jesus is called Muhammad's "Lord" (Koran 89:22) and the Truth (Koran 2:91). The Koran also describes Jesus as the "Word" of God (Koran 3:45; 4:171) and a "spirit proceeding from Him" (Koran 4:171).

The Connection Between Islam and Culture

Islam is far more than a religion. It is an all-encompassing way of thinking. It is a culture and a system of government. To ensure his political preeminence, Muhammad spoke about rewards—economic and spiritual—for those who fight and die for the Islamic faith and moral code. In the Bukhari Hadith (*Sahih al-Bukhari*), regarded as the most trustworthy of all the extra-Koranic traditions or Hadiths, Muhammad is quoted as saying, "Allah assigns for a person who participates in [holy battles] in Allah's Cause . . . that he will be recompensed by Allah either with a reward, or booty [if he survives] or will be admitted to Paradise [if he is killed in the battle as a martyr]."[6]

Muhammad developed a form of theocratic government that pertains to all aspects of life. He began with the conduct of dissidents, the treatment of allies, the formation of treaties, and other political matters. Later, elements of a code of conduct and moral law were introduced.

Toward the end of his life, Muhammad began to clarify his aspirations for the future of Islam. He made a silver seal engraved with the words "Muhammad, the apostle of God" and sent four simultaneous messages bearing this stamp to the rulers of Egypt, Abyssinia, Syria, and Persia. He urged them to forsake their idols and to believe in the universal faith of God's message given through him, God's messenger.

In launching this appeal to the nations, Muhammad sought to export not only the religion of Islam but also the culture of Islam—a distinctly Arab culture. Throughout the Muslim world, Arab culture is considered the ideal expression of Islam. Algeria's first president, Ahmed Ben Bella, once said, "I cannot see Arab culture separate from Islamic culture. I honestly would not understand the meaning of Arab culture if it were not first and foremost Islamic." [7]

This alignment between the Arab culture and Islam runs deep in the hearts and minds of the Arab people. It is one of the foremost reasons that fanatical Muslims are deeply angered when their Arab countrymen adopt Western cultural behaviors, such as a preference for Western dress or Western styles of entertainment. To the Arab Islamic mind, Western culture is anti-Islamic, and thus anathema (or cursed) to Arabs.

People sometimes ask why Muslims are so adamant about head coverings, such as the *burka* and *chador* for women or the turban-style coverings for men. The answer: these head coverings were popular in the Arabic culture for thousands of years, largely as protection against the blowing desert sands. When Islam became the religion of Arabia, the dress of Arabia became an expression of Islam. Whether a person lives in the cold mountains of Afghanistan or the jungles of Indonesia, to be a Muslim means to dress like Arabs.

The Death of the Prophet

When Muhammad was in his early sixties, and Islam was only twenty years old, the self-proclaimed "apostle of God" fell ill with a sudden fever and died. As news of his death spread, many Muslims were seized with panic and confusion. Abu Bakr, Muhammad's close friend (and the first Islamic caliph), declared to Muhammad's distraught followers, "Those of you who worshiped Muhammad know that he is dead, but those of you who worshiped God [Allah] know that he is alive."[8]

Muhammad's goal was to create a society in which religion encompassed all aspects of the culture and daily life. The goal of Islamic leaders today is still a complete blend of the Islamic religion and Arab culture with a goal of absolute world domination.

FOUR

Are Allah and Jehovah
the Same God?

D URING WORLD WAR I, English mathematician
Bertrand Russell was sentenced to six months in
prison for writing anti-war articles for a pacifist magazine,
The Tribunal. In his autobiography, Russell recalled the day he
surrendered himself at the prison gate to begin his sentence.
The warden at the gate, who filled out the paperwork, asked
Russell his religion.

"Agnostic," Bertrand Russell replied.

"Could you spell that, please?" the warden asked.

Russell spelled it.

The warden wrote it down, then said, "Well, there are many
religions, but I suppose they all worship the same God."[1]

Agnostics aside, is it true that all religions worship the
same God? Like Judaism and Christianity, Islam is a monotheistic religion—but is the Allah of Islam the same God
as Jehovah, the God of Judaism and Christianity? What do
Muslims actually believe about the deity they call Allah?

These are vitally important questions, and few Christians know the truth about the Muslim concept of Allah.

Who Is Allah?

Monotheism—belief in one God—is central to Islamic doctrine. Muslims do not understand the Christian concept of the Trinity, in which we worship one God who exists as three persons: Father, Son, and Holy Spirit. Muslims think Christians worship three gods, not one. This misconception goes back to Muhammad himself. In the Koran, he sometimes refers to Christians as polytheists (or, depending on the translation, idolaters) because of their belief in the Trinity.

The Koran gives ninety-nine attributes of Allah. These are called the "most Beautiful Names." Many are names that Christians are familiar with: the All-Powerful, the Creator, the Merciful, the Compassionate. The essence of Allah, however, is power. His power overrides all of his other attributes.

You may have heard Muslim apologists claim that Islam is "the religion of peace," suggesting that the word *Islam* comes from the Arabic word *salaam*, meaning "peace." But anyone with even the most elementary knowledge of the Arabic language knows this is not true. *Islam* derives from the Arabic word *aslama*, which means "total surrender" or "total submission," especially to God. The word suggests a vanquished army on its knees in surrender before a powerful conqueror. The word *Islam* suggests the power of Allah to conquer all opponents.

The name Allah comes from pre-Islamic times, and it corresponds to the Babylonian name Bel or Baal. According to Middle East scholar E. M. Wherry, pre-Islamic Arabs worshipped gods they called Allah. Both pre-Islamic Allah-worship and Baal-worship involved worship of the sun, the moon, and the stars, which is why they are called astral religions. The crescent moon, the symbol of pagan moon worship, is also the symbol of Islam. It is printed on the flags of many Islamic countries and placed atop minarets and mosques.[2]

How Is Allah Different from Jehovah?

What is Allah's character like? Islam describes Allah as being neither wholly a spirit nor a physical entity, but an entirely separate form of being, remote, aloof, and distant. By contrast, Jehovah, the God of Judaism and Christianity, is portrayed in the Old and New Testaments as continually seeking a relationship with humankind. He walked and talked with Adam and Eve in the Garden of Eden. He told the people of Israel, "You will be my people, and I will be your God" (Jeremiah 30:22; see also Genesis 17:7–8; Exodus 6:7).

The Koran presents Allah as being forever hidden from humanity. The Bible presents Jehovah as drawing near and seeking us out. The first question we find in the Bible is God calling to Adam and Eve, "Where are you?" (Genesis 3:9). In the Koran, Allah hides from humanity. In the Bible, humanity hides from God.

Though Allah is described as all-powerful, Islam requires Muslims to take revenge whenever Allah is insulted. The

God of the Bible never makes such demands. We Christians don't avenge God—He avenges us. While Muslims are commanded to fight for Allah, the God of the Bible says that He will fight for us (Exodus 14:14; 2 Chronicles 20:7; Psalm 28:7; Isaiah 49:25).

Jesus taught us that instead of beheading our enemies, we are to pray for our enemies, do good to them, and "turn to them the other cheek" when they mistreat us (Matthew 5:39). We don't demand that unbelievers convert to Christ at the point of a sword. We appeal to unbelievers to accept God's mercy and forgiveness through Christ (2 Corinthians 5:20). If they reject our gospel, we don't slay them—we pray for them and love them.

If Allah and Jehovah are the same God, why does Allah speak and act so differently from the God of the Bible?

Islam claims that the angel Gabriel revealed Allah's will to Muhammad. In other words, Gabriel gave the human race, through Muhammad, a set of instructions. Gabriel did not give Muhammad any insight into the nature, character, or personality of Allah. That is why the Allah of the Koran remains hidden and mysterious, whereas the God of the Bible is personal and knowable. Jehovah God revealed Himself to Abraham, whom He called friend (James 2:23). God conversed with Moses, revealing His name to Moses— "I am" (Exodus 3:14).

The God of the Bible reveals Himself to humanity by telling us His names—names that describe His character and attributes. Here are just a few of God's names, along with the attributes those names describe for us:

Adonai (Lord, Master)

El Shaddai (Lord God Almighty)

El Elyon (The Most High God)

El Olam (The Everlasting God)

Jehovah Gmolah (The Lord Who Recompenses)

Jehovah Jireh (The Lord My Provider)

Jehovah Mekoddishkem (The Lord Our Sanctifier)

Jehovah Nissi (The Lord My Banner)

Jehovah Raah (The Lord My Shepherd)

Jehovah Rapha (The Lord Who Heals)

Jehovah Sabaoth (The Lord of Hosts)

Jehovah Shalom (The Lord Is Peace)

Jehovah Shammah (The Lord Is Present)

Jehovah Tsidkenu (The Lord Our Righteousness)

How Do Muslims Relate to Allah?

Islam and Christianity present very different pictures of how humanity should relate to Allah or God. Both Islam and Christianity call for people to accept *by faith* what God has revealed. There is no disagreement about the need for faith. There is vast disagreement, however, when it comes to what has been revealed.

Islam says that the ultimate truth was revealed by Allah to Muhammad through the angel Gabriel. Muslims contend that the Bible in its present form is corrupt and that only the Koran contains the true divine message.

Christians believe that ultimate truth was evident in the life of Jesus Christ, who said, "I am the way and the truth and the life. No one comes to the Father except through me" (John 14:6). Jesus revealed God's truth by His life as the incarnate Son of God. He is the Logos, the Word of God, the full expression of God's character, truth, and love toward humanity (John 1:1–3, 14).

Muslims view the issue of sin very differently from Christians and Jews. At first glance, we see that much of what the Koran says about sin is roughly similar to what the Bible says. The Koran uses several words for *sin* that suggest the idea of failing to meet God's standards.

Islam states that human beings were created for the service of Allah. That service includes absolute obedience to what Allah commands. Therefore, says Islam, the root of sin lies in humanity's prideful opposition to God's will. Humanity is prone to wrong actions because human beings are morally weak. Therefore, it is up to human beings to choose to be strong and to do good works. If they obey Allah, their good works will counterbalance their evil works. The Koran teaches, "For those things, that are good remove those that are evil" (Koran 11:114).

Muslims believe Allah has given to all people the ability to obey. Therefore, human beings only need to be guided into obedience. The Koran does not view the sin of Adam and Eve as having caused humanity's fall, so Islam has no doctrine of original sin or a sin nature. Instead, Islam classifies various misdeeds as being great or small for the purpose of determining the degree of punishment to be meted out.

"Little sins" (*saghira*) include lying, deception, anger, and lust. Such sins are easily forgiven if the greater sins are avoided and if compensatory good works are performed. In fact, a lie may actually be a good deed if it helps someone or advances the cause of Islam.

"Great sins" (*kabira*) include murder, adultery, disobeying God, disobeying one's parents, drinking to excess, practicing usury, neglecting Friday prayers, not keeping the fast of Ramadan, swearing by any name other than Allah's, performing magic, gambling, dancing, or shaving one's beard. Such sins can be forgiven only after repentant deeds.

Acts the Bible recognizes as sexual sins—adultery and fornication—are often labeled in the Koran as acts of "temporary marriage" rather than sin (Koran 4:3–34). *Nikah mut'ah* (temporary marriage) is an arrangement recognized in Shia Islam by which a man and woman can be married for a fixed, temporary period of time. Students or workers who are away from home may marry for a period of days, weeks, or months so that their needs for companionship and sex may be met. When that period of time is over, the marriage is dissolved without divorce. The man often makes a payment to the woman called a *mahr* (or dower). Sometimes a brief temporary marriage can serve as a fig leaf for legalized prostitution, but it is not considered a sin.

The sin that surpasses all others in Islam is *shirk*, the association of other deities with Allah. The sin of shirk is unpardonable. According to tradition, Muhammad was asked to identify the greatest sin, and he said it was polytheism or idolatry, the worship of more than one deity. Muslims believe that Christians are guilty of polytheism, and thus Christians are guilty of the unpardonable sin of shirk. This is all a Muslim needs to justify a holy war against Christians, whom they view as unbelievers who have corrupted true monotheistic faith.

What Does Allah Do About Sin?

The Muslim view of Allah is that of an elderly, grandfatherly Arab gentleman who is pleased when people obey him—and infuriated when they disobey. Allah rewards or punishes according to his mood. To the faithful, Allah is the Lord of blessing and bounty, but like a benevolent dictator he insists on total compliance with his laws.

That's a key reason that democracy is so rare in the Islamic world. In Iraq and Afghanistan, democracy has been imposed by the United States in the aftermath of war—and the future of democracy in those lands is uncertain. The only other Islamic democracy is Turkey, a nation that embraced secularism following the collapse of the Ottoman Empire in 1923. The increasingly theocratic policies of Turkish prime minister Recep Tayyip Erdoğan have placed Turkish democracy in doubt.

Like Islam itself, Islamic governments tend to be dictatorial and authoritarian. The Muslim view of Allah is intertwined with the Arab view of leadership, which holds that a ruler must be an absolute monarch or dictator. A ruler whose powers are constitutionally limited does not fit the Islamic view of power. A limited ruler appears weak. In Islam, *a ruler must rule*, rewarding those who please him and punishing those who disobey.

Yet Muslims also believe that Allah can be merciful if he chooses. He accepts repentance and forgives faults and shortcomings. Every chapter of the Koran but one opens with the words, "In the name of Allah, the Most Beneficent, the Most Merciful." Muslims believe that every word and accent in the Koran reveals the mercies of Allah.

The Koran teaches that human beings must seek forgiveness from Allah because he is all-knowing. Here we see another similarity to the God of the Bible. Allah sees the secrets of the heart—nothing escapes his notice. It is Allah's *maghfera* (forgiveness) that preserves and protects a person from Allah's wrath and punishment. The Koran proclaims repeatedly that Allah forgives sins, but here we see an important distinction between Islam and Christianity: Muslims believe Allah is remote and unknowable, so there is no way a human being can have the assurance of forgiveness. There is no promise of grace and forgiveness in the Koran as there is in the Bible.

Judaism and Christianity teach that human beings have a sin nature from birth, and that sin must be cleansed. For the Jews, Jehovah provided a means of atonement through the blood sacrifices of the Law. For Christians, the ultimate atoning sacrifice was the death of Jesus on the cross, which was foreshadowed by the Old Testament sacrifices.

But Islam provides no atonement for sin. There are no sacrifices pointing to an atoning Messiah, as in Judaism. There is no atoning blood of Christ to cover the sins of a believer once and for all. There is no assurance of salvation in Islam as there is in the Christian gospel. Though Allah is called "merciful" in the Koran, he dispenses mercy or punishment according to his whim.

The Islamic View of Jesus

The incarnation of Christ is a major stumbling block for Muslims. Christians believe that Jesus is God's Son, that He is God in human flesh. Muslims reject the idea that God has taken human form in order to dwell among us and experience the human condition.

Muhammad, influenced by the pagan idolatry of pre-Islamic Arabia, mistakenly thought that Christians believed God had married a human woman and produced a son by her. Myths of gods having sexual relations with human beings and producing superhuman offspring are common in polytheistic religions. Muhammad rejected these crude, pagan beliefs—and rightly so.

Because of Muhammad's illiteracy and limited contact with Christian theology, he mistakenly thought that Christians believed the Trinity was composed of God, Jesus, and Mary. Many Muslims hold this misconception today.

Islam views Jesus (Isa) as a prophet of God. The Islamic religion accepts Jesus' miracles. The Koran calls Christians and Jews "People of the Book" because their religions are based on revealed Scripture. (Muslims view the Koran itself as the completion of the revelation that was begun in the Old and New Testaments.) But Muslims do not believe Jesus was God in human flesh.

Islam not only denies that Jesus is the Son of God but pronounces a curse on all who confess Jesus to be the Christ, the Son of God, and the Lord of all. The Koran says, "The Jews call 'Uzair [Ezra] a son of Allah, and the Christians call Christ the son of Allah. That is a saying from their mouth; (in this) they but imitate what the unbelievers of old used to say. Allah's curse be on them: how they are deluded away from the Truth!" (Koran 9:30). In Islam, Allah's curse is tantamount to a death sentence.

One of the aspects of Christianity most difficult for Muslims to grasp is the cross of Christ. The purpose of the cross eludes Muslims because they see no need for a sacrifice for sin. Moreover, the idea of substitutionary atonement for sin is, to their minds, primitive. Though Muslims do not abhor the shedding of blood, they reject the notion that there is virtue in dying for someone else. Muslims will die to advance Islam, but they would not die for the sake of fellow Muslims. A Muslim cannot comprehend the highest expression of love, when Jesus took the penalty for our sins upon Himself.

Islamic teaching about Jesus renders meaningless His substitutionary death on the cross. Muslims don't believe Jesus died on the cross. They believe that when the Roman soldiers came to Jesus by night in the Garden of Gethsemane, God took Jesus up into heaven before the soldiers even laid hands on Him. Therefore, Jesus was never crucified, did not shed His blood, and did not die. He ascended directly to heaven.

Islamic scholars offer different theories as to who was actually crucified. Some say that Judas Iscariot was crucified in Jesus' place, and others suggest Simon of Cyrene, who carried the cross of Jesus for a while. Another theory is that one of the disciples volunteered to be crucified in Jesus' place. Each theory involves the idea that the likeness of Jesus was supernaturally transferred to the man who died in Jesus' place.

The Bible teaches that Jesus voluntarily humbled Himself and submitted to death on the cross out of love for us. In Islam, by contrast, that kind of self-sacrificing love is seen as a sign of weakness. To love is to be vulnerable. Far be it from Allah, the all-powerful, to be vulnerable! Islam has no concept of the strength of love.

How Islam's View of Allah Affects Muslims' Behavior

How we relate to God is generally how we relate to others. Muslims are taught to view the giving of alms (charitable donations) as a religious duty, not a heartfelt act of compassion and love for others. Muslims are taught to judge, condemn, and even exterminate those who fail to measure up to the highest standards of faith and religious practice. Why? Because that is how they expect Allah to deal with them if they disobey his commands.

Islam is curiously similar to the pre-Islamic tribal religions that Muhammad rejected. It focuses on an outward show of obedience to Allah, not an inward attitude of love toward Allah. In Islam, there is no recognition of God's goal (repeatedly expressed in both the Old and New Testaments) of reestablishing a love relationship with the human race.

If the Koran truly completes the revelation of the Bible, as Muslims believe, then why does the Koran contain no hint of the divine love that permeates the Old and New Testaments?

In Islam's zeal to give praise to Allah's power, it underestimates the *real* power of God, which is the power of divine love. Muslims cannot comprehend the love that compelled God to take human form and live humbly as a man among men so that all might know who God is and what God is like. Muslims cannot grasp the love relationship and friendship between God and His people that is at the heart of the Christian faith. As Jesus told His disciples, "I no longer call you servants, because a servant does not know his master's business. Instead, I have called you friends, for everything that I learned from my Father I have made known to you" (John 15:15). The theme of friendship and fellowship with God is completely absent from the Koran.

A Muslim's Greatest Hope: To Avoid Allah's Wrath

Muslims ask, "How could God enter into human life and remain God?" That's a good question. As the apostle Paul told Timothy, this very issue—the fact that God was made visible in human form—is the mystery of godliness, the baffling truth at the heart of our faith (1 Timothy 3:16). This mystery is impossible for Muslims to accept.

To the Muslim mind, the Christian assertion that we are created in God's image is blasphemy. This mind-set, of course, constitutes a rejection of the creation story of Genesis. To

Muslims, the creation of humanity was an act of Allah's absolute power, and Allah created us not to have fellowship with him but simply to serve him. Human beings are required to submit to the divine will, which Allah exercises arbitrarily as he pleases, according to his infinite power.

According to the Koran, Allah often misleads and deceives people, based on his own whim. This notion of a deity who capriciously deceives people is completely unlike the Judeo-Christian Jehovah. Our God does not mislead us—that would violate His nature. "Guide me in your truth," prays the Psalmist (Psalm 25:5). "God is truthful," says the apostle John (John 3:33). God's judgment, said Paul, "is based on truth" (Romans 2:2). The Spirit of God, the Bible tells us, is "the Spirit of truth" (1 John 4:6). Though God will permit those who reject the truth to sink deeper into their own self-willed, self-made delusion (Ezekiel 14:9–11; 1 Kings 22:19–23; 2 Thessalonians 2:10–12; James 1:13–16), the Scriptures tell us clearly that "it is impossible for God to lie" (Hebrews 6:18; see also Titus 1:2).

Adherents to Islam are not invited into a relationship with Allah. Instead, Muslims are commanded to practice religious rites and duties (Koran 30:30). Muslims' motivation is not a love for the Creator but a fear of punishment.

In Islamic theology, humanity was created in a state of moral goodness but is prone to stray when tempted. Even so, according to Islam, humanity is not radically estranged from God and our fundamental nature is not sinful.

In sharp contrast, Christians believe the Fall radically damaged human nature. Though we were made in God's image, we became lost in sin, alienated from God, and incapable of pleasing God through our own works. Though we are fallen, our original purpose remains the same: We were created to have fellowship with our loving God, and He has restored that broken relationship through Christ. By His death upon the cross, Jesus saved us, redeemed us from sin and death, and fulfilled our longing for a meaningful life. By dying in our place, Jesus enables us to reflect again God's image on this earth.

These precious truths are incomprehensible to Muslims, who cannot imagine a life of fellowship with Allah. The most any Muslim can hope for is to avoid Allah's wrath.

A Side-by-Side Comparison of Islam and Christianity

	Islam	Christianity
1. Allah/God	Distant (unknowable). Does not reveal himself, reveals only his will. Merciful (depending on his mood). Capricious (he leads and misleads). Vengeful. Almighty (emphasis on power).	Personal (knowable). Reveals Himself through the incarnation of Jesus Christ. Loving (His love is unchanging). Truthful. Just and loving. Almighty (power balanced by love).
2. Christ	A prophet. Not God incarnate.	God's Son. The Word made flesh.
3. Bible	Revealed by God. Changed and corrupted by unfaithful Jews and Christians.	Revealed by God. Authoritative Word of God.

	Islam	Christianity
4. Trinity	God, Jesus, and Mary (Islam's distorted version)	Father, Son, and Holy Spirit; One God in three persons
5. Faith	Intellectual agreement that Allah is One and Muhammad is his Prophet.	Recognition that we are sinners and unable to save ourselves; we trust in Christ's substitutionary payment (atonement) for our sins.
6. Sin	Rebellion against God. Result: shame, embarrassment. Dishonor to family. People are inherently good. We are absolved by good works.	Rebellion against God (primarily). Result: guilt. Requires God's forgiveness. People are inherently fallen. The penalty of sin is death; Jesus paid the penalty for our sin.
7. Salvation	God saves those whom he chooses. Faith and works are required. We cannot be assured of salvation.	Salvation is available to all who believe. Our works cannot save us. All who believe in Jesus will be saved.

	Islam	Christianity
8. Sanctification	Based on rituals and obedience to the Koran. Keep the Five Pillars of Islam. External and ceremonial.	Based on our growth toward Christlikeness through the work of the Holy Spirit. Inward, spiritual, based on a living relationship with God.
9. Love	Islam recognizes erotic love and family love. Self-sacrificing love is seen as weakness.	Highest form of love is Christlike, self-sacrificing, *agape* love. Family love, friendship love, and erotic love have their place, but secondary to *agape* love.
10. Belief in Supernatural	Belief in unseen world. Angels (good and evil). Satan is a force of hate and power. Islamic belief is fatalistic; all events are foreordained by Allah.	Belief in spiritual realm. Belief in angels and demons as described in the Bible. Satan is the rebellious archenemy of God, completely evil, but his power is no match for God's power. Human beings can overcome evil only through the power of God that is supplied by the Holy Spirit.

FIVE

What Does Islam Teach About the End Times?

As we compare the widely differing views of Islam and Christianity, two observations become clear: First, Islam has adopted and distorted bits and pieces of the Old and New Testaments. The Koran retells stories from the Old and New Testaments in a fractured form, presents a distorted image of God, and depicts Jesus (Isa) as neither Savior nor Son of God. Second, despite superficial similarities, Islam and Christianity differ radically in how they portray the character of God, the nature of Jesus Christ, and God's relationship to humanity.

Where do these differences lead? They lead to completely opposite prescriptions for living—and very different views of the end times.

Islamic Belief about the Afterlife

Muslims believe that Allah decrees everything that happens, including birth and death. The Koran teaches that man's hour of death is ordained: "If Allah were to punish men for their wrong-doing, He would not leave, on the (earth), a single living creature: but He gives them respite for a stated Term: When their Term expires, they would not be able to delay (the punishment) for a single hour, just as they would not be able to anticipate it (for a single hour)" (Koran 16:61). Only Allah knows exactly when the Last Judgment will come: "They ask thee about the (final) Hour—when will be its appointed time? Say: 'The knowledge thereof is with my Lord (alone): None but He can reveal as to when it will occur'" (Koran 7:187).

Islamic belief divides the afterlife into heaven and hell—a division that appears superficially to be similar to Christian belief. In heaven, according to Islam, believers experience God's favor and benevolence. In hell, unbelievers experience God's judgment and wrath. Both destinations are vividly described in the Koran.

In Islam, heaven is an oasis-like paradise filled with rivers of milk, wine, clarified honey, and shade trees bearing all kinds of fruits. In hell, sufferers will be made to drink boiling water, molten metal, and decaying filth. The Koran says, "Those who are wretched shall be in the Fire: There will be for them therein (nothing but) the heaving of sighs and sobs" (Koran 11:106). The Islamic hell has seven divisions, each with its particular purpose and terrors. For example, there is a Muslim purgatory, a special division of hell for Christians, a division for Jews, and a bottomless pit for hypocrites. Many details of the Islamic heaven and hell stand in stark contrast with the teachings of the Bible.

L. Bevan Jones, in *The People of the Mosque*, describes the Muslim concept of the Day of Judgment. According to Islamic doctrine, the Last Day will not come until there is no one remaining who calls on Allah. Then the trumpet will sound, announcing the Day of Judgment, which will unfold this way:

1. At the first trumpet blast, everyone in heaven and earth will die except those God saves.

2. At the second trumpet blast, the dead will be resurrected.

3. After the resurrection, there will be a forty-year period when people will wander about the earth naked, confused, and sorrowful. They must await the reading of the books that have been kept by the recording angels. Each book will be given to its owner, delivered into the right hand of the righteous and into the left hand of the wicked.

4. Everyone's deeds will be weighed on Allah's scales of justice (Koran 21:47). The scales weigh each one's good deeds and bad deeds, and the fate of each individual is determined. Good deeds are heavy; bad deeds are light. Those whose balance is light will lose their souls and go into hell (Koran 23:102–103; 101:6–11). Prophets and angels are exempt from this trial and (according to some Islamic authorities) so are believers.

5. After one's deeds are weighed, the next step is to cross the bridge over hell. Jones wrote, "The Prophet [Muhammad] is reported to have said: 'There will be a bridge sharper than the edge of a sword, finer than a hair, suspended over hell.' Some will pass over it in the twinkling of an eye, some like a flash of lightning, others with the speed of a swift horse. The angels will call out, 'O Lord, save and protect!' Some Muslims will be saved, some will fall headlong into hell, and afterwards be released. The infidels will all fall into hell and remain there for ever."[1]

In Islam, the promise of eternal life is always linked to good works. The Koran records twenty-four times that Allah has no love for sinners and that he loves only those who fear him. The Christian concept of salvation for sinners is completely unknown in Islam. Those who fail to live as the Koran instructs have only damnation and everlasting torment to look forward to.

The Antichrist versus the Mahdi

The Bible refers to a particular individual called "the antichrist" (1 John 2:18, 22; 4:3; 2 John 1:7). Elsewhere in the Bible, the Antichrist is known by various names. Paul calls him "the man of lawlessness," "the man doomed to destruction," and "the lawless one" who "will exalt himself over everything that is called God or is worshiped, so that he sets himself up in God's temple, proclaiming himself to be

God" (2 Thessalonians 2:3, 8, 4). The most detailed description of the Antichrist is in Revelation 13, where the apostle John refers to the Antichrist as "the beast" (v. 3). The Old Testament prophet Daniel describes the abominable works of the Antichrist but gives him no name or title (Daniel 9:27).

Jesus refers to Daniel's prophecy of the Antichrist in the Olivet Discourse. The disciples ask Jesus, "What will be the sign of your coming and of the end of the age?" (Matthew 24:3). He tells them:

> So when you see standing in the holy place "the abomination that causes desolation," spoken of through the prophet Daniel—let the reader understand—then let those who are in Judea flee to the mountains. Let no one on the housetop go down to take anything out of the house. Let no one in the field go back to get their cloak. How dreadful it will be in those days for pregnant women and nursing mothers! Pray that your flight will not take place in winter or on the Sabbath. For then there will be great distress, unequaled from the beginning of the world until now—and never to be equaled again. (Matthew 24:15–21)

Who, then, is the Antichrist, whose brief but terrible reign is predicted in both the Old and New Testaments? He will be a world leader of unparalleled political, military, and religious power. He will be charming, persuasive, and popular beyond measure. The world will not know him as the "Antichrist" but by some attractive name and appealing title. But just as the word *Antichrist* suggests, he will be the opposite of the Lord Jesus Christ in every way. Everything Christ is, the Antichrist is not; everything Christ is not, the Antichrist is.

Jesus came from heaven (John 6:38); the Antichrist comes from the Abyss, the spiritual domain of evil (Revelation 11:7). Jesus came in the name of the Father; the Antichrist comes in his own name (John 5:43). Jesus was despised by the world (Isaiah 53:3); the Antichrist is worshipped by the world (Revelation 13:3–4). Jesus came in humility as a servant (Philippians 2:7–8); the Antichrist comes in pride, claiming to be God (2 Thessalonians 2:4; Daniel 11:36). Jesus is the truth (John 14:6); the Antichrist is the lie (2 Thessalonians 2:9–11). Jesus is the Son of God (Mark 1:1; Luke 1:35); the Antichrist is the son of perdition (2 Thessalonians 2:3 KJV).

The apostle Paul tells us that the mystery (or secret) of godliness is that God Himself has appeared to us in human flesh (1 Timothy 3:16)—and that the secret (or mystery) of lawlessness is that Satan has produced a counterfeit Christ, the Antichrist, Satan wrapped in human flesh (2 Thessalonians 2:6–8). Jesus is the true Shepherd; Satan will have his evil shepherd, the Antichrist. Jesus is the Holy One of God; the Antichrist will be the lawless one of Satan. Jesus is the Man of Sorrows; the Antichrist will be the man of sin.

Interestingly, Islamic teaching about the Last Days predicts the rise of a powerful leader strikingly similar to the Christian's Antichrist. In Islam, this prophetic figure is called the Mahdi. Muslims see the Mahdi as a savior who will lead a global revolution and establish a worldwide Islamic empire. The Mahdi will rule the earth as the final Caliph of Islam (a caliph is both a political ruler and a spiritual representative of Allah on earth).

The Mahdi—the prophesied redeemer and savior of Islamic eschatology—will appear on the scene at the same time as the return of Jesus. As L. Bevan Jones notes, "the Mahdi is to be a man of war whose path will be red with the blood of 'unbelievers.'"[2]

Muslims revere Jesus (whom they call Isa) as the *Masih* or Messiah. In Islamic eschatology, the Mahdi will arrive at the same time that Isa returns. Isa will descend to earth in Syria, east of Damascus, dressed in yellow robes, and will assist the Mahdi, who will rule over the earth for seven years (or, in some Islamic traditions, nine or nineteen years). At the end of the Mahdi's rule, there will be a Day of Judgment for the entire human race.

In Sunni Islam, the Mahdi is the successor of Muhammad who will arise to rule the world and establish righteousness. In Shia Islam, the Mahdi is identified as "the Twelfth Imam." Muhammad al-Mahdi, who was born in the ninth century, became an imam at age five, and he supposedly vanished at age seventy-one in an event called "the Occultation." He is said to be alive but hidden until Allah reveals him and sends him forth to bring justice to the world.

The parallels between the biblical Antichrist and the Mahdi of Islam are chilling. Both are associated with the end times and the Judgment. Both possess political, military, and religious power, and both head up a one-world religion. The Mahdi will force all non-Muslim people to convert to Islam. Like the Antichrist, the Mahdi will establish Jerusalem as his capital, from which he will rule the earth. Islamic scholars Muhammad ibn Izzat and Muhammad Arif write:

> The Mahdi will be victorious and eradicate those pigs and dogs and the idols of this time so that there will once more be a caliphate based on prophethood as the hadith states. . . . Jerusalem will be the location of the rightly guided caliphate and the center of Islamic rule, which will be headed by Imam al-Mahdi. . . . That will abolish the leadership of the Jews . . . and put an end to the domination of the Satans who spit evil into people and cause corruption in the earth, making them slaves of false idols and ruling the world by laws other than the Sharia [Islamic law] of the Lord of the worlds.[3]

Though Muslims revere Jesus as a prophet, they deny that Jesus is the Son of God. Jews and Christians are, to Muslim fundamentalists, "pigs and dogs" who must either convert to Islam or be eliminated. Bible prophecy makes it clear that the Antichrist will target Jews and Christians for destruction, just as Islamic prophecy states that the Mahdi will wage war against Jews and Christians. Those who oppose the Antichrist's worldwide religion will be executed.

Muslim scholar Imam Muhammad Baqir states clearly how the Mahdi will establish his one-world religion: "There must be bloodshed and jihad to establish Imam Mahdi's rule." And Ayatollah Ibrahim al Amini of the Religious Learning Center in Qom, agrees: "The Mahdi will offer the religion of Islam to the Jews and Christians; if they accept it, they will be spared, otherwise they will be killed."[4]

Radical Islamists believe the Mahdi will shed the blood of infidel "pigs" and "dogs," and they look forward to that time with rejoicing. Christians believe the Antichrist will shed the blood of God's chosen people, God's saints—and they feel sorrow and compassion for those who will have to endure those days.

Jesus Himself said, "For then there will be great distress, unequaled from the beginning of the world until now—and never to be equaled again. If those days had not been cut short, no one would survive, but for the sake of the elect those days will be shortened. . . . See, I have told you ahead of time" (Matthew 24:21–22, 25).

The Old Testament prophet Daniel tells us (and Jesus affirms in the Olivet Discourse) that the Antichrist will establish "the abomination that causes desolation" in the temple in Jerusalem (Daniel 9:27). The apostle Paul adds that the Antichrist "will oppose and will exalt himself over everything that is called God or is worshiped, so that he sets himself up in God's temple, proclaiming himself to be God" (2 Thessalonians 2:4). Since the temple was destroyed in AD 70, as Jesus predicted, this has led some to suggest that the Jewish temple must be rebuilt on the Temple Mount before the Antichrist can be revealed to the world.

The Dome of the Rock and the al-Aqsa Mosque stand on the Temple Mount today. One of the Islamic Hadiths (traditions) records that the Prophet Muhammad said, "[Armies carrying] black flags will come from Khurasan [Iran and Afghanistan], no power will be able to stop them and they will finally reach Eela [the al-Aqsa Mosque in Jerusalem] where they will erect their flags." In Islamic tradition, black banners symbolize violent conquest, and Muslims await the Mahdi's conquest of Jerusalem, when he establishes his reign from the temple site.

Daniel 9:27 tells us the Antichrist will establish a seven-year covenant with Israel—but he will break the covenant after three and a half years, defiling the temple with "an abomination that causes desolation." The Hadiths of Islam also speak of a seven-year covenant that the Mahdi makes with Israel: "The Prophet said: There will be four peace agreements between you and the Romans. The fourth will be mediated through a person who will be from the progeny of Hadrat Aaron [Honorable Aaron, the brother of Moses] and will be upheld for seven years."[5]

There can be no doubt: Satan is preparing Muslims to accept the Mahdi as their leader—and the Mahdi is indistinguishable from the world leader we know as the Antichrist.

When this counterfeit "redeemer" arises to impose his bloody reign upon the world, the people of the Islamic world, sadly, will be well prepared to receive him and follow him to hell itself. We are already getting a foretaste of that future through the ceaseless campaign of terror now being waged against us.

One Antichrist and Many Antichrists

In 1 John 2:18, the apostle John tells us, "Dear children, this is the last hour; and as you have heard that the antichrist is coming, even now many antichrists have come." What does John mean?

He is telling us, first of all, that the Antichrist is coming—a lawless man who will come in Satan's power, demanding to be worshipped as God, destroying all those who love God. But John is also telling us that there are many other antichrists, lesser deceivers who are also self-exalting, evil, and destructive. They are antichrists, but they are not *the* Antichrist.

Jesus tells us that shortly before His return, the Antichrist will arise during a time of global chaos and confusion, when the world is in political, social, financial, and ecological upheaval. The terrified people of the world, desperate for a strong leader, will turn to this man and give him control of the governments of the world.

Daniel tells us that the Antichrist will speak "boastfully" (Daniel 7:8), yet it is clear that these will not be empty boasts. The Antichrist will appear to possess superhuman brilliance. He'll be the ultimate smooth talker, the greatest con man who ever lived, and he'll unite the nations under his rule. At first, he'll seem to be a wise and benevolent dictator, bringing peace, prosperity, and hope. But once he is firmly in control of the gears and levers of power, he'll reveal his true intentions.

The way has been paved for such a leader. Atheists, humanists, New Age mystics, Hindus, Buddhists, and Islamists have little in common with one another—but they all agree that Jesus is *not* the only way to salvation. There are even many self-styled "Christians" who deny the Lord's claim to be the only way to God.

In 2004, a rising young politician named Barack Obama gave an interview to Chicago *Sun Times* columnist Cathleen Falsani. When Falsani asked, "What do you believe?" he replied:

I am a Christian.

So, I have a deep faith. So I draw from the Christian faith.

On the other hand, I was born in Hawaii where obviously there are a lot of Eastern influences.

I lived in Indonesia, the largest Muslim country in the world, between the ages of six and ten.

My father was from Kenya, and although he was probably most accurately labeled an agnostic, his father was Muslim.

And I'd say, probably, intellectually I've drawn as much from Judaism as any other faith.

This sounds at first like a typical appeal-to-all-sides answer: he states, "I am a Christian," but he adds that he has also been shaped by Eastern influences, a Muslim background, and Judaism. He goes on to explain why he calls himself a Christian:

> I'm rooted in the Christian tradition. I believe that there are many paths to the same place, and that is a belief that there is a higher power, a belief that we are connected as a people. That there are values that transcend race or culture, that move us forward, and there's an obligation for all of us individually as well as collectively to take responsibility to make those values lived.[6]

It's laudable to transcend race and recognize that we are all connected in the human family. But when Obama says, "there are many paths to the same place," he is not speaking as a Christian. He is not speaking from Christian tradition or the Christian Scriptures. He is, in fact, contradicting Jesus.

The statement "there are many paths to the same place" comes not from Christianity but from the spirit of this dying age, the spirit of antichrist, which denies that Jesus is the way and the truth and the life. Please understand me and don't misquote me: I am not saying that President Barack Obama is the Antichrist. I'm saying his thinking reflects the antichristian spirit of this age, which claims to affirm Jesus while denying His claim to be the only way to God the Father.

The Christian message is not an inclusive message that embraces all religions; it's not a message that there are many paths to the same place. The Christian message is summed up in the brave words of Peter before the Sanhedrin: "Jesus is 'the stone you builders rejected, which has become the cornerstone.' Salvation is found in no one else, for there is no other name under heaven given to mankind by which we must be saved" (Acts 4:11–12).

The Big Lie

One of the great tragedies of the evangelical church today is that many professing Christians have bought the Big Lie that all religions lead to God. According to the Barna Group, a California-based polling organization, fully one-quarter of self-described "born-again Christians" believe that all people will eventually be saved and accepted into heaven, even without faith in Jesus Christ. Roughly the same proportion, 26 percent, believe that religion doesn't matter because "all faiths teach the same lessons." Forty percent said they believe "Christians and Muslims worship the same God."[7]

I have a few questions for those "born-again Christians" who see no need for anyone to be born again: If people can be saved and accepted by God the Father apart from the saving work of Jesus Christ on the cross, then why was He crucified? What does Jesus' sacrifice on the cross mean if you can be saved without it? And if there are many ways to heaven apart from Christ, what does that make Jesus, who claimed to be the *only* way to heaven? Doesn't that make Him a liar?

For centuries, Satan has prepared humanity to accept the Big Lie: *You don't need Christ. You can be saved without Him.*

It doesn't matter what you believe, as long as you're sincere. There are many religions, many paths, but they all lead to the same God. Satan has deluded most of the human race, including many professing Christians. He has convinced the human race that Jesus is irrelevant to salvation and that it doesn't matter whether you believe in Him or not.

Talk show host Oprah Winfrey once interviewed a woman who claimed to have had a near-death experience. The woman said she died, left her body, and encountered Jesus. She told Oprah that, while she was "dead," Jesus revealed to her that "all religions are equally true."

Oprah replied, "I believe that there are many paths to God. Or, many paths to the light. I certainly don't believe that there is only one way. . . . Did Jesus indicate that to you?"

"Yes," the woman said, "absolutely."

"Well," Oprah said, "I'm glad to hear that because if Jesus is as cool as I think He is, He would have had to tell you that."[8]

In Oprah's opinion, the "cool" Jesus would contradict the Jesus of the Bible. But the real Jesus would never say one thing through Scripture and the opposite thing through a woman on a TV show. Jesus does not contradict Himself. He is the same yesterday, today, and tomorrow. Anyone who claims that Jesus says all religions are equally true is not speaking for Christ. That person is delivering the deceptive message of an antichrist.

To be a genuine Christian, you must believe the claims of Christ. You must confess that salvation comes by grace through faith in the crucified Lord Jesus, and not by any other means. You must believe that Jesus is the way and the truth and the life, just as He said. If you profess otherwise, you are antichristian in your thinking.

When you surrender to antichristian thinking, you place yourself in spiritual danger. If you reject the truth that Jesus alone is the way and the truth and the life, you leave yourself open to the great end-times delusion. When the Antichrist comes in all his deceptive power, your mind and heart will be unprotected. The Antichrist will seem to be a savior—and you may even mistake the Antichrist for the second coming of Christ Himself.

Many people who think themselves wise—including many in the church!—will be fooled by the Antichrist. His words will be more subtle and persuasive than you could ever imagine. People around you will be praising and worshipping him, and you may be fooled into joining them. You may think you would recognize the Antichrist if you saw him—but you'd probably be wrong. Jesus warned, "False messiahs and false prophets will appear and perform great signs and wonders to deceive, if possible, even the elect" (Matthew 24:24).

The apostle Paul also warns us against being deceived by the Antichrist. He writes, "Don't let anyone deceive you in any way, for that day will not come until the rebellion occurs and the man of lawlessness is revealed, the man doomed to destruction. He will oppose and will exalt himself over everything that is called God or is worshiped, so that he sets himself up in God's temple, proclaiming himself to be God" (2 Thessalonians 2:3–4).

No one knows the day or the hour of the Lord's return, but we do know that this prideful con man, the Antichrist, will attract followers who will worship and praise him as if he were God. Once he has solidified his hold on the governments of the world, he will turn against God's people and betray them. He will set himself up as God in the temple of Jerusalem and demand to be worshipped. He will commit "the abomination that causes desolation," as Jesus warns in Matthew 24:15 (referring to the prophecies in Daniel 9:27, 11:31, and 12:11), and he will perform counterfeit miracles and wonders—an evil parody of the miracles of Christ.

In the book of Revelation, we see that the Antichrist ("the beast") will fake his own death and resurrection in order to convince the masses that he is the Christ. The Antichrist will suffer a seemingly fatal wound and be miraculously healed, causing the whole world to worship him and follow him (Revelation 13:3–4). This seemingly miraculous power comes from Satan, who needs to possess a human body as his visible representative on earth. The Satan-possessed Antichrist will do Satan's bidding in opposing God and persecuting His people.

Four Indisputable Facts About Bible Prophecy

Bible scholars—many of whom are good friends of mine and deeply committed students of God's Word—have varying views about the order and timing of future events. After studying these different views, I have become convinced of four indisputable facts about Bible prophecy:

1. Only those who receive Jesus Christ as Savior and Lord will be welcomed into heaven.
2. Jesus is coming back as He repeatedly promised.
3. There will be a judgment upon those who have rejected Jesus as the only way to heaven.
4. When Jesus appears, all true believers will go to be with Him.

That's all I need to know. It really doesn't matter to me whether I go through the Tribulation or I don't go through it. It doesn't matter whether I see the Antichrist or I'm removed from this world before the Antichrist is revealed. When I trusted Jesus for my salvation, I trusted Him with my eternal future. How He chooses to unfold the future is entirely up to Him.

Wherever Jesus is, that is heaven for me. The One who created this beautiful planet said He has prepared an even *more* beautiful place for all who love Him. Jesus promised that where He is, His followers will also be (John 14:3). No matter what happens in the future, He will neither leave us nor forsake us (Deuteronomy 31:6). We have His word on that. As the apostle Paul assures us, "For I am convinced that neither death nor life, neither angels nor demons, neither the present nor the future, nor any powers, neither height nor depth, nor anything else in all creation, will be able to separate us from the love of God that is in Christ Jesus our Lord" (Romans 8:38–39).

Theologians can speculate endlessly about the meaning of various prophetic symbols or the order of prophetic events. But ultimately, the most important fact to understand about the Antichrist is that his defeat is certain. In the fullness of time, Jesus, the true Christ, will appear and destroy the Antichrist, consigning him to the eternal fires (Daniel 7:11, 21–22; 17:26; 2 Thessalonians 2:8; Revelation 2:16; 19:20). The Lord Jesus and His people will emerge victorious—and that's all that matters.

In the meantime, believers continue to follow Christ and spread His good news as we await His return. The Antichrist (with a capital *A*) has not yet been revealed—but we live amid many antichrists (with a small *a*), false teachers and false preachers who claim that there are many paths, many religions, but they all lead to the same God. There are many (small *a*) antichrists who tell us that it doesn't matter what we believe, as long as we are sincere. There are many (small *a*) antichrists who tell us that it is intolerant and unkind to tell people that Jesus is the only way to God the Father. There are many (small *a*) antichrists who tell us that the second coming of Christ is merely a symbol or metaphor and that Jesus will not physically return to reign.

I don't want you to be deceived. The spirit of antichrist is already in the church, and the Bible repeatedly warns us not to be taken in by the antichristian deceivers who have infiltrated our fellowship. The apostle John tells us, "Even now many antichrists have come" (1 John 2:18). Peter warns, "There will be false teachers among you. They will secretly introduce destructive heresies, even denying the sovereign Lord" (2 Peter 2:1). And Paul reminds us to beware of "false apostles, deceitful workers, masquerading as apostles of Christ" (2 Corinthians 11:13).

Jesus said, "If you hold to my teaching, you are really my disciples. Then you will know the truth, and the truth will set you free" (John 8:31–32). The truth that sets us free is this: Jesus is the one and only way to everlasting life.

SIX

Two Different Prescriptions for Life

ENTREPRENEUR STEVE JOBS was one of the most brilliant men of our age, often compared to Thomas Edison
and Walt Disney. But in October 2003, Steve Jobs made an
error in judgment that almost certainly shortened his life by
many years.

His doctors told him he had a malignant tumor in his pan-
creas. While the prognosis for most forms of pancreatic cancer is
poor, Jobs had a rare form of pancreatic cancer—islet cell carci-
noma—that is one of the least aggressive types of cancer. When
caught early, as Jobs's tumor was, it is quite treatable. With surgery, Jobs had an excellent chance of making a full recovery.

But Jobs rejected his doctors' recommendation and chose
to treat his cancer with a self-prescribed combination of
fruit juices, acupuncture, visits to New Age spiritualists, and
various other pseudoscientific treatments he found on the
Internet. For the next nine months, Jobs ignored the pleas of
his doctors, family, and friends.

Finally, Steve Jobs realized he was following the wrong prescription and he wasn't getting better. He belatedly agreed to undergo surgery and employ the most advanced cancer-fighting therapies available—though, by that time, the tumor had grown larger and the cancer had spread to the surrounding tissues. Doctors managed to extend Jobs's life for another eight years beyond the original diagnosis, but they believe Jobs would have beaten the cancer if he had allowed them to remove the tumor when it was first discovered.

Why did such a brilliant man reject scientifically proven cancer treatments in favor of out-and-out quackery and voodoo medicine? Jobs's biographer, Walter Isaacson, explained that Jobs felt that "if you ignore something you don't want to exist, you can have [what you desire through] magical thinking. . . . He would regret it."[1] In every arena of life, from our physical health to our spiritual health, it's vital to follow the right prescription. In the medical realm, the wrong prescription can cost you your mortal life. In the spiritual realm, the wrong prescription can cost you your eternal life.

Christianity and Islam are two very different spiritual and moral prescriptions. They are as different as surgery and acupuncture, or chemotherapy and fruit juice. If you want to know God, if you want to experience His peace and power in your life, if you don't want to suffer the pain of everlasting regret, then you must choose the right spiritual prescription.

The Christian prescription is a faith that brings you into a personal relationship with the God of the universe. The Christian faith sets you free from guilt, shame, and bondage to sin. Genuine biblical Christianity does not impose itself on unwilling people at the point of a sword. If you choose to reject Jesus, you're perfectly free to do so. As the apostle Paul writes, "Now the Lord is the Spirit, and where the Spirit of the Lord is, there is freedom" (2 Corinthians 3:17).

The reason we have freedom of religion written into the First Amendment to the Constitution is that the American government was designed by people who believed in God. They came from many Christian faith traditions. They were Congregationalists, Presbyterians, Episcopalians, Roman Catholics, Deists, and more—and they believed in freedom of worship, both their own freedom and the freedom of their neighbors.

Islam, by contrast, is a religion of law, submission, and punishment. The ideal world, according to Islam, is one that strictly obeys every tenet of Islam, with no separation between religion and state. The ideal political leader, to the Islamic mind, is an iron-fisted Islamic caliph. The edicts of religion, the Muslim believes, should be enforced with the power of the state—the power of the sword. There should be no tolerance for other religions. Religion and the state should be one and the same.

The Islamic faith offers no loving God, no assurance of forgiveness or salvation, no power over sin, no newness of life, no personal relationship with the Creator, no freedom from guilt, no freedom of any kind. Where the Spirit of the Lord is, there is freedom; but where Islam reigns, there is fear. Islam and Christianity offer totally different prescriptions for living. And the wrong prescription can be deadly.

The Christian Prescription

The most basic prescription for Christian living is summed up in two simple commandments, voiced first in Judaism and reaffirmed by Jesus: "'Love the Lord your God with all your heart and with all your soul and with all your mind.' This is the first and greatest commandment. And the second is like it: 'Love your neighbor as yourself.' All the Law and the Prophets hang on these two commandments" (Matthew 22:37–40; see also Deuteronomy 6:5).

Do Christians universally obey these simple commandments? Tragically, no.

All too many professing Christians display an unloving spirit—unloving toward God and unloving toward their neighbors. Christians are not immune to self-righteousness, prejudice, anger, and bitterness. But there is nothing in Christianity that condones unloving attitudes or behaviors. Authentic Christians constantly strive, with the help of God, to weed out habits or behaviors that hinder the expression of God's love in their lives.

The clear command of Jesus to His followers is still, "Love each other as I have loved you" (John 15:12). Christians continually fall short of Christ's example. The history of Christianity is riddled with horrifying failures: the Crusades, the anti-Jewish pogroms, the Spanish Inquisition of the Middle Ages, and the recent bloody history of Northern Ireland. As genuine Christians, we are ashamed of these events that dishonor the gospel.

Jesus told us that we are to be known by our love. As John wrote, "This is the message you heard from the beginning: We should love one another. Do not be like Cain, who belonged to the evil one and murdered his brother" (1 John 3:11–12). And, "This is how we know what love is: Jesus Christ laid down his life for us. And we ought to lay down our lives for our brothers and sisters. . . . Dear children, let us not love with words or speech but with actions and in truth" (1 John 3:16, 18).

The message of God's love toward us rings loud and clear throughout the Gospels. Jesus said, "For God so loved the world that he gave his one and only Son, that whoever believes in him shall not perish but have eternal life. For God did not send his Son into the world to condemn the world, but to save the world through him" (John 3:16–17).

Jesus also said, "Love your enemies, do good to those who hate you, bless those who curse you, pray for those who mistreat you. . . . Love your enemies, do good to them, and lend to them without expecting to get anything back. Then your reward will be great, and you will be children of the Most High, because he is kind to the ungrateful and wicked. Be merciful, just as your Father is merciful" (Luke 6:27–28, 35–36).

The ancient Greeks had four separate words for four distinctly different kinds of love. There is *philia,* or friendship love; *storge,* or family love; *eros*, romantic love or the love of beauty; and finally there is *agape*, the highest love of all—a Christlike, self-sacrificing love that is rooted not in the emotions, but in the will. *Agape* love is the decision to keep loving and seeking the best for someone even when we don't feel like it, even when that person sins against us.

When Jesus says, "Love your enemies," He is speaking of *agape* love. You can't have loving feelings toward people who hurt you, but you can *choose* to love your enemies through a deliberate act of your will. That's the love God has shown to you and me, and that's the love Jesus commands us to demonstrate to one another.

Muslims frequently point to the Crusades and the Inquisition as two great stains on Christian history—and with justification. After capturing Jerusalem in 1099, the Crusaders slaughtered innocent men, women, children, Muslims, Jews, and even other Christians. Though Islamic historians have exaggerated the death toll, there can be no justification for what the Crusaders did in the name of Christ.

In 1994, Pope John Paul II issued an apology for the actions of the Crusaders and called the atrocities they committed departures from the Spirit of Christ and His gospel. It was right for him to do so.

But will Muslims ever issue an apology for what Muslim armies did against Christians and Jews? Not likely. The spread of Islam in the Middle Ages took place primarily through military conquest, not voluntary conversions. The history of Islam is one of massacres, enslavement, torture, and brutality far exceeding the crimes of the Crusaders.

The gospel of Jesus Christ challenges us to confess our faults, to seek and give forgiveness, and to love our neighbors and our enemies. There is no equivalent to these Christian duties in Islam. The Koran commands Muslims to wage war on the unbelievers, to conquer them, and if need be, to annihilate them.

Christians are to win their enemies over through love, compassion, and Christlike acts of charity. The prescription of *agape* love, confession, and forgiveness is central to the Christian life. It is unknown in Islam.

The Prescription of Islam

In contrast to Christianity, Islam is a religion of law, blind submission, fear, and punishment. Under an Islamic theocracy, submitting to the ruler is the equivalent to submitting to Allah. Islam doesn't simply require belief; Islam demands surrender and submission.

A Bedouin tribe in seventh-century Arabia professed faith to Muhammad, saying, "We believe in Allah!" Muhammad is said to have replied, "Ye have no faith; but ye (only) say, 'We have submitted our wills to Allah'" (Koran 49:14).

A Muslim's fundamental religious duties and beliefs are summed up in the Five Pillars of Islam:

1. *Confession of Faith (Shahadah)*. This means reciting the statement, "There is no god but Allah, and Muhammad is the Messenger of Allah."
2. *Prayer*. Formal prayers must be recited five times a day: before sunrise, after midday, at midafternoon, shortly after sunset, and in the fullness of night. Prayer

involves kneeling and prostrating oneself in the direction of Mecca.

3. *Paying the Alms Tax (Zakat).* The legal zakat, or "purification tax," is levied on property. All Muslims pay this religious tax for the benefit of the poor (which may include one's own family members, the needy, and at times, the poor stranger who is passing through the area). The amount of the *zakat* is predetermined—usually about two and a half percent of one's wealth. In some circumstances, the percentage may be higher.

4. *Fasting and Prayers at Ramadan.* Fasting is generally limited to the holy month of Ramadan, the month in which Muslims believe the first verses of the Koran were revealed to Muhammad in AD 610. Between sunrise and sunset, adult Muslims do not smoke, eat, drink, or engage in sexual intercourse. They may eat and drink only between sunset and sunrise. Ramadan is both the name of the ninth month on the Islamic calendar (a lunar calendar), and the name of the period of religious observance marked by fasting. The three days that follow Ramadan are a time for feasting, almsgiving, and exchanging gifts.

5. *Pilgrimage (Hajj).* Every Muslim of sound mind and body who can afford the journey is expected to make a pilgrimage, called Hajj, to Mecca at least once in a lifetime. Those who make the pilgrimage may add al-Hajj to their names.

These five duties are the minimal obligations of every good Muslim. In addition to the Five Pillars, Muslims are expected to "commend good and reprimand evil" and they are forbidden to gamble, to charge interest on loans to fellow Muslims, or to consume alcohol or pork. Islam is a religion of rituals and external behaviors that one must carry out to receive Allah's favor.

Christians may be tempted to regard Islamic belief as "salvation by works." Salvation, however, is not an Islamic doctrine. Because Islam does not view humanity as having a sinful nature, people do not need to be saved. Muslims live in fear of offending Allah and suffering an eternity in hell. Muslims experience spiritual anxiety because they can never be assured of having done enough good deeds and rituals to earn Allah's approval.

When Muslims pray to Allah, they employ a certain amount of cajoling and begging. Five times a day, they bow before this unknowable deity. A constant sense of insecurity, and even dread, is integral to Islam. In Islam, there is no parable of the unmerciful servant (Matthew 18:21–35), no statement of "Forgive, and you will be forgiven" (Luke 6:37), no forgive-us-as-we-forgive-others principle, as in the Lord's Prayer (Luke 11:4). Because Muslims see Allah as unyielding and vengeful, they tend to interact with others in a judgmental, unforgiving way.

Islam's prescription focuses on outward rituals and works. Christianity's prescription is focused on the believer's heart.

What About Those Who Don't Believe?

Christianity regards nonbelievers as "unconverted." Jesus commissioned His followers to preach His good news throughout the world and give every person an opportunity to accept Him as Lord and Savior. That's the essence of Christian evangelism.

By contrast, Islam regards nonbelievers as "infidels." The word *infidel* comes from the same root as *infidelity*, the act or condition of being unfaithful. To Muslims, nonbelievers are not merely people who do not believe. They are faithless and treacherous. They are enemies of the faith. Muslims do not seek to spread the "good news" of Islam, because Islam has no "good news" to spread—no grace, no forgiveness, no peace with God. Muslims seek only to bring the world into subjection to Islam. Subjection does not require free will. A person can be *forced* to surrender to Allah, willing or not.

This is a critical distinction. It lies at the heart of the Islamic terrorism we have witnessed. Many Westerners ask, "Why are Muslims so fanatical about their religion? Why is it that the more devout a Muslim is, the more intolerant he tends to be toward other religions?"

Muslims believe they alone have been given the final revelation of God in the Koran. Muslims respect the Torah (the five books of Moses) and the Injeel (their version of the gospel). But their sacred book, the Koran, teaches that they are called to enforce God's will. The Koran calls upon all Muslims to convert or conquer unbelievers. For those who take the Koran seriously, there is no room for moderation or tolerance.

Islamic law is the core of Islamic thought. Islamic scholars may disagree on how various laws should be implemented, but there is little disagreement about one central idea: non-Muslims do not belong to the House of Islam (*Dar al-Islam*); therefore, they belong to the House of War (*Dar al-Harb*). In simple language, if you aren't with us, you're against us. Infidels are to be humiliated, oppressed, denied legal protection, and ultimately coerced into conversion or killed.

The Koran says clearly and forthrightly, "Fight those who believe not in Allah nor the Last Day, nor hold that forbidden which hath been forbidden by Allah and His Messenger, nor acknowledge the religion of Truth, (even if they are) of the People of the Book, until they pay the Jizya [religious tax] with willing submission, and feel themselves subdued" (Koran 9:29). No genuine Christian would pursue such a warlike strategy against non-Christians. It would go against all the teachings of Jesus. But a commitment to a warlike strategy is what defines a deeply committed Muslim. Islamic zealots consider even moderate Muslims to be "infidels."

There are only three ways to deal with non-Muslims under Islamic law: They must be converted, they must be subjugated and humiliated, or they must be eliminated (except women, children, and slaves). Islamic law distinguishes between types of non-Muslims; Christians and Jews are in different categories from other non-Muslims.

Some Islamic governments permit an "infidel" to enter into a formal agreement or treaty that spares the unbeliever's life and property. Such non-Muslims are classified as *dhimmi* ("people of the *dhimma*" or "people of the contract"). A dhimmi is granted limited rights and responsibilities under Sharia law and is subjugated by the Islamic state. A dhimmi must wear identifiable clothing and live in a specially marked house. He must not ride a horse. He must always yield the right-of-way to Muslims. A dhimmi cannot be a witness in a legal court except in matters relating only to other dhimmis. He cannot be the guardian of a Muslim child, the owner of a Muslim slave, or a judge in a Muslim court.[2]

What does all this mean to us in the West? Dhimmi is the classification given to Christians in Muslim countries. These are the restrictions under which Christians must live and work. In fact, this is how the Saudi government treated our soldiers when they went to defend Saudi Arabia from Saddam Hussein during the Gulf War. If you understand how Christians are required to live in Islamic nations, you'll understand better how to pray for your Christian brothers and sisters who are serving in Muslim nations.

Most non-Muslims are not regarded as citizens by any Islamic state, even if they are original natives of the land. That is why Muslim extremists in such countries as Egypt, Syria, Lebanon, and even Iraq—where Christians are somewhat tolerated—want to topple these regimes. They do not consider these nations to be full-fledged Islamic states unless non-Muslims are given second-class status.

When a nation declares itself to be an Islamic state by law, its native non-Muslim people are reduced to second-class status. The history of Egypt gives us an excellent example of how this works.

The Islamic religion first came to Egypt in the middle 600s. The onslaught of Islam was strongly resisted by the Coptic Church, which was founded around AD 42 by Mark the Evangelist, the author of the second Gospel. The Coptic Church had six centuries in which to become established and strong before Muslims from Arabia overran Egypt. The price of resisting Islam and refusing to convert was often death. Those who were not martyred lived under heavy taxation.

Today in Egypt, the Copts have retained much of their original heritage. About 10 percent of Egypt's more than eighty-five million people are Christians, and the vast majority of them are Copts.[3] Life has always been precarious for the Copts. If the Muslim Brotherhood and other Islamist groups in Egypt get their way, the government will come under Sharia law and return to the concept of dhimmi, which would turn the Copts into second-class citizens in the land where they have lived for almost two thousand years.

For decades, the Muslim Brotherhood has targeted Egyptian Copts for violence. The Egyptian Christians have been beaten, maimed, and killed. Their property is often confiscated or destroyed. Waves of violence pass through the land like a paroxysm of hate, targeting Christian shops, restaurants, homes, and churches.

Westerners, steeped in the tradition of separation of church and state, find it difficult to imagine what life is like for Coptic Christians in Egypt. Many Westerners do not understand that Muslims cannot imagine a separation between religion and state. In the Muslim mind, the state is an extension of the religion. Muslims assume that religion and government are intertwined, even in America. So when America gets involved in events in the Middle East, Muslims do not see America as a secular government but as a Christian "Crusader" nation. To the Islamic mind, it's as if it's still the eleventh century and the Crusades are still going on.

That's why Osama bin Laden, in his 1996 fatwa, "Declaration of War against the Americans Occupying the Land of the Two Holy Places," refers more than twenty times to "the American Crusader forces" (the US military) or "the Zionist-Crusader alliance" (Israel and the United States).[4] Bin Laden seemed oblivious to the fact that "the American Crusader forces" have actually defended Muslims against the Soviets in Afghanistan, against the Serbs in Bosnia, against the Iraqis in Kuwait, and on and on. Would a "Crusader" nation spend American lives and American wealth to protect Muslims? The notion makes no sense.

The Muslim view of America is irrational and delusional. But that delusion drives many of the bloody events of recent history—and history will only get bloodier as radical Islamists continue their efforts to subjugate the world in the name of Islam and Allah. That delusion drives a concept that has profoundly affected everyday life in America and around the world.

It is a concept known as *jihad*.

SEVEN

What Is Jihad?

I N EARLY 2013, citizens of San Francisco and Chicago were startled to see huge placards on city buses, with smiling Middle Eastern–looking people and the word *Jihad* in big red letters. One sign read, "My Jihad is to build friendships across the aisle. What's yours?" Another read, "My Jihad is to not judge people by their cover. What's yours?" Another showed a.young Muslim woman in a hijab, a Muslim headscarf, lifting a barbell and saying, "My Jihad is to stay fit despite my busy schedule. What's yours?"[1]

The bus ads were the work of CAIR, the Council on American-Islamic Relations, a Muslim advocacy group headquartered in Washington, DC. Though it portrays itself as a "civil liberties" organization, CAIR has documented ties to the terrorist organization Hamas[2] and the Muslim Brotherhood (CAIR's founders, Nihad Awad and Omar Ahmed, were members of the Brotherhood's Palestine Committee in America).[3]

CAIR claims that the "My Jihad" ad campaign is intended to educate Americans about the "real" meaning of the word *jihad*.[4] But the campaign actually appears more intended to confuse than educate. CAIR's attempt to rebrand *jihad* as a warm and fuzzy concept triggered an immediate backlash.

Pamela Geller, executive director of the American Freedom Defense Initiative, posted look-alike ads that satirized the CAIR ads. Geller's ads showed Osama bin Laden, Fort Hood shooter Nidal Hasan, the World Trade Center exploding on 9/11, and other jihad-related images. One featured a quote by Turkish prime minister Recep Tayyip Erdoğan: "The mosques are our barracks, the domes our helmets, the minarets our bayonets, and the faithful our soldiers," along with the ironic tagline "That's My Jihad. What's yours?" Another showed a hooded Palestinian terrorist saying, "Killing Jews is worship that draws us close to Allah," and, "That's My Jihad. What's yours?"

Geller explained, "Our new ads depict actual jihadists carrying out their own jihads and is a truth antidote to CAIR's deceptions. . . . It is reprehensible to put a happy face on mass murder, ethnic cleansing, honor violence and religious persecution."[5]

What is the truth about jihad?

The Struggle

The first word Palestinian schoolchildren learn in their reading primers is *jihad*. It is often the first word shouted as mobs of radical Muslims assault Coptic Christians in Cairo or Alexandria. It is the first word on the lips of those who plot terror attacks against the West.

The word *jihad*, often associated with Islamic "holy war," literally means "struggle." There are three types of jihad recognized by Muslim scholars. First, there is the kind of jihad described in the CAIR ads—the inner struggle of maintaining self-discipline and battling evil in one's heart. Though CAIR would have us believe this is the most common definition of jihad, it is a relatively uncommon usage among Muslims.

Second, there is the jihad against Satan—the struggle against temptation and spiritual oppression. Christians would call it "spiritual warfare," struggling against the attacks of Satan. This, too, is a fairly uncommon usage of the term.

Third, there is the jihad against infidels, unbelievers, and hypocrites—the fight against all who reject or oppose Islam. This form of jihad is often violent, which is why many radical Islamic organizations have the word *jihad* in their name— Osama bin Laden's International Islamic Front for the Jihad Against Jews and Crusaders, for example, or the Palestinian Islamic Jihad.

The Islamic Hadith (traditions) consists of several collections of sayings attributed to Muhammad. One of these collections, the Bukhari Hadith (*Sahih al-Bukhari*), is considered the most trusted and authentic Islamic text next to the Koran itself. An analysis of the text indicates that 97 percent of references to jihad in the Bukhari Hadith refer to warlike jihad against unbelievers. Only 3 percent refer to jihad as an inward spiritual struggle.[6]

The struggle for the victory of Islam is central to the life of every faithful Muslim. Even those who see jihad as a personal religious term must acknowledge that, down through the centuries, Muslims have regarded jihad as the struggle for

Islam to gain preeminence over all other religions. Muslim Brotherhood founder Hasan al-Banna explained it this way:

> How wise was the man who said, "Force is the surest way of implementing the right, how beautiful it is that force and right should march side by side." This striving to broadcast the Islamic mission, quite apart from preserving the hallowed concepts of Islam, is another religious duty imposed by God on the Muslims, just as he imposed fasting, prayer, pilgrimage, alms, and the doing of good and abandonment of evil, upon them. He imposes it upon them and delegated them to do it. He did not excuse anyone possessing strength and capacity from performing it.[7]

Jihad, according to Islamic law, must be waged until the Day of Judgment. Islam allows no permanent peaceful coexistence with infidels. Jihad is an essential ingredient of Islamic philosophy, and all who truly love the Koranic faith are devoted to jihad. It's the hook on which hang all rationales for the use of political power and force to advance the Islamic cause.

Though the concept of mercy appears in the Koran, there is no room for mercy toward those who oppose the advance of Islam. The Koran states, "But when the forbidden months are past, then fight and slay the Pagans wherever ye find them, and seize them, beleaguer them, and lie in wait for them in every stratagem (of war); but if they repent, and establish regular prayers and practise regular charity, then open the way for them: for Allah is Oft-Forgiving, Most Merciful" (Koran 9:5). And, "O Prophet! strive against the disbelievers and the Hypocrites, and be firm against them. Their abode is Hell, an evil refuge indeed" (Koran 9:73).

Are All Fundamentalists the Same?

Some have drawn a moral equivalence between fundamentalist Islam and fundamentalist Christianity, as if both are equally dangerous. When Rosie O'Donnell was a cohost of ABC's *The View*, she said, "Radical Christianity is just as threatening as radical Islam in a country like America."[8] A similar view is expressed by highly respected Harvard divinity professor Harvey Cox. In a column in the *Boston Globe*, Cox lumps Protestant, Catholic, and Muslim fundamentalism together and tries to draw a moral equivalence between them:

> As the twentieth century ended and a new one began, fundamentalism has taken on more formidable shapes, both politically and religiously. Though most of its adherents work through spiritual and educational channels, the small minority that turn to violence have caught the media's attention. If some seem ready to die for faith, others are ready to kill for it, gunning down abortion doctors in church, hijacking planes, and exploding bombs at weddings. For plenty of thoughtful people, fundamentalism has come to represent the most dangerous threat to open societies since the fall of communism.[9]

An example Cox offers of the "threat" of Christian fundamentalism is the phrase "gunning down abortion doctors in church"—and that is misleading. There has only been one abortion doctor shot in church (not "doctors" plural), and the gunman who shot Dr. George Tiller in Kansas had been diagnosed with mental illness. Professor Cox would like to equate the Tiller murder to 9/11, but the facts don't fit.

A Christian fundamentalist is simply not the equivalent of a Muslim fundamentalist. If a Christian hijacked a plane and flew it into a building, he or she would be violating the Scriptures at every point—there is not one verse of the Bible that would justify such an act.

But the Koran presents Islam as a militant faith: "Slay the Pagans wherever ye find them . . ." (Koran 9:5); "Fight the unbelievers who gird you about, and let them find firmness in you" (Koran 9:123). In the Hadith, Muhammad says, "I have been ordered to fight against all the people until they testify that there is no god but Allah and that Muhammad is Allah's messenger, and offer the prayers perfectly, and give the obligatory charity. So if they perform all that, then they save their lives and property from me and their reckoning will be done by Allah."[10] In *Answering Islam*, Norman Geisler writes,

While many Muslims are peace-loving, nonetheless, those who commit acts of violence and terror in the name of God can find ample justification for their actions, based on the teachings of the [Koran] and the sayings and examples from prophet Muhammad himself. . . . Christians who have engaged in violence are betraying the explicit teachings and examples of Jesus Christ. On the other hand, Muslims who take upon themselves to destroy their alleged enemies in the name of God can rightly claim to be following the commands of God in the [Koran] and imitating their prophet as their role model. . . .

The minority groups in Islam who resort to violence are not an aberration to Islam but in fact can legitimately claim to be working within the basic parameters of Islamic Jihad.[11]

Within the Muslim world, a power struggle rages between radical, militant Muslims and moderate Muslims. Radical Islam can never coexist with the voices of moderation. The goal of fundamentalist Islam is total fidelity to the most extreme and militant passages of the Koran—and those passages demand domination of the world and subjugation of all non-Muslims. Moderates, in the eyes of the radicals, are only one step removed from being non-Muslims, because they stand in the way of Islam's absolute supremacy.

The shout of the radical always drowns out the voice of moderation.

Washing Blood with Blood

An ancient Middle Eastern saying states, "Wash blood with blood." In other words, when your enemy draws blood, be prepared to spill more blood, both his and yours. We hear the command to wash blood with blood in these statements by prominent Islamic leaders:

- In 1983, just one week after the bombing of the Marine barracks in Beirut, Lebanon, Sheikh Muhammad Yazbeck said, "Let America, Israel, and the world know that we have a lust for martyrdom and our motto is being translated into reality."[12]

- Hussein Musawi, leader of the Islamic Amal movement, said, "This path is the path of blood, the path of martyrdom. For us, death is easier than smoking a cigarette if it comes while fighting for the cause of God and while defending the oppressed."[13]

- Hasan al-Banna, the founder of the Muslim Brotherhood of Egypt, told his followers, "You are not a benevolent organization, nor a political party, nor a local association with limited aims. Rather, you are a new spirit making its way into the heart of this nation, and reviving it through the Koran; a new light dawning and scattering the darkness of materialism through the knowledge of God; a resounding voice rising and echoing the message of the Apostle [Muhammad]."[14]

- Shukri Ahmed Mustafa, a leader of the Muslim Brotherhood offshoot group *Jama'at al-Muslimin* (Society of Muslims), told a reporter before he was hanged in 1978, "Spilling the blood of heretics is the sacred duty of all Muslims."[15] Mustafa hoped that, through acts of violence, he could prod the masses toward a full-scale Islamic revolution that would result in an "Islamic Republic of Egypt"—a first step toward the global Islamic Caliphate.

Some Americans believe that by rounding up hundreds or thousands of al-Qaeda fighters, we can end Islamic terrorism. But this would be like washing blood with blood. No matter how many terrorists you kill, there are always more lining up to take their place. Though the War on Terror is critically important in restraining the jihadist onslaught, war alone is not the answer. We must also fight for the hearts and minds of those who would do us harm.

Stealth Jihad

Ayaan Hirsi Magan Isse Guleid Ali Wai'ays Muhammad Ali Umar Osman Mahamud (yes, that's her full name) was born in Mogadishu, Somalia. After her father was imprisoned for opposing Somali dictator Siad Barre, Ayaan was raised by her grandmother. When Ayaan was five years old, she underwent a traumatic ordeal. She recalls:

In Somalia . . . little girls are made "pure" by having their genitals cut out. There is no other way to describe this procedure, which typically occurs around the age of five. . . .

Female genital mutilation predates Islam. . . . But in Somalia, where virtually every girl is excised, the practice is always justified in the name of Islam. . . .

My father was a modern man and considered the practice barbaric. He had always insisted that his daughters be left uncut. . . . [But while he was in prison], Grandma decided that . . . the old traditions would be respected in the old ways.[16]

So Ayaan Hirsi Ali underwent ritual genital mutilation at the age of five. Growing up, she attended Saudi-funded Islamic schools and became fanatically committed to following the Koran. She wore the hijab, supported the Muslim Brotherhood, and wanted to be a good Muslim. After moving to the Netherlands and attending Leiden University, her faith in Islam gradually eroded.

She was in her early thirties at the time of the 9/11 attacks. She saw televised videotapes of Osama bin Laden justifying the attacks on the basis of the Koran. He spoke of total war on America and Israel, and Ayaan thought his words sounded "like the ravings of a madman." His quotes from the Koran and the Hadith troubled her: "When you meet the unbelievers, strike them in the neck." "If you do not go out and fight, God will punish you severely and put others in your place." "Wherever you find the polytheists, kill them, seize them, besiege them, ambush them." "The Hour [of Judgment] will not come until the Muslims fight the Jews and kill them."

Ayaan searched the Koran and the Hadith and found the passages bin Laden had quoted. "I didn't want to question [the word of Allah]. . . ," she wrote, "but I needed to ask: Did the 9/11 attacks stem from true belief in true Islam? And if so, what did *I* think about Islam?"[17]

The questions led her to become an outspoken critic of Islam, the religion she had formerly embraced. She opposed the subjugation of women under Islamic law, including the practice of "honor killings," in which Muslim parents kill their children for refusing an arranged marriage, wearing inappropriate dress, having premarital sex, or even being the victim of rape. She was outspoken against the practice of female genital mutilation.

Ayaan helped produce a short film called *Submission*, which denounced the oppression of women in Islamic society. Two months after it aired on Dutch TV, the film's producer, Theo van Gogh, was shot and slashed to death by a Dutch-Moroccan Islamist. The killer pinned a note on van Gogh's body, promising to kill Ayaan Hirsi Ali next.

She went into hiding for a few months and then began making public appearances, refusing to be silenced by threats. In 2005, she was named one of the hundred most influential people in the world by *Time* magazine. She now lives in the United States and works with the American Enterprise Institute in Washington, DC, and Harvard's Kennedy School of Government.

In 2014, Brandeis University announced that Ayaan Hirsi Ali would give a commencement address and receive an honorary degree. Almost immediately, the university came under pressure from the Muslim Brotherhood–related Council on American-Islamic Relations (CAIR) and the Muslim Student Association, which denounced Ayaan's views as "outright Islamophobic."[18] Since *Islamophobia* literally means "fear of Islam," it could be argued that Ayaan Hirsi Ali has much to fear from a religion that mutilated her and threatened her life.

But "Islamophobia" is merely a label that radical Muslims use to silence and intimidate anyone who disagrees with them. Muzzling opposing views is a form of jihad, a way of waging holy war against the non-Muslim world without resorting to bombs or bullets. And it works. Faced with protests and pressure from radical Muslims, Brandeis University withdrew its invitation for Ayaan Hirsi Ali to speak.

Universities were once places where all points of view could be discussed, where intellectual freedom reigned, where young people could flex their critical-thinking skills. Today, universities are places where open-mindedness is no longer tolerated, and where an aggrieved Muslim minority can shout down any point of view it dislikes. Brandeis is a prime example of how universities are becoming willing accomplices in squelching free speech, oppressing women and girls in the Islamic world, and advancing what I would call a "stealth jihad" agenda for America.

Islam has a name for this "stealth jihad" strategy—a strategy of moving into non-Muslim cultures and then applying pressure to make them bow to Islamic law. This "stealth jihad" strategy is called *dawah*. In a broad sense, *dawah* means to issue a summons or invitation, and it refers to inviting non-Muslims to convert to Islam. A person who practices dawah is called a *da'i*—a Muslim missionary.

But there is also a clandestine form of dawah that is focused on moving into a non-Muslim culture, infiltrating that culture, and forcing it to become subservient to Islamic law. Mohamed Akram (aka Mohamed Adlouni) described the "stealth jihad" aims of Islam in a May 1991 memo he wrote for the Shura Council of the Muslim Brotherhood. The memo, which was written in Arabic, referred to a "long-term plan . . . approved and adopted" by the Shura Council in 1987. It describes the long-term plan this way:

> The process of settlement is a "Civilization-Jihadist Process" with all the word means. The Ikhwan [Brotherhood] must understand that their work in America is a kind of grand Jihad in eliminating and destroying the Western civilization from within and "sabotaging" its miserable house by their hands and the hands of the believers so that it is eliminated and God's religion is made victorious over all other religions. . . . It is a Muslim's destiny to perform Jihad and work wherever he is and wherever he lands until the final hour comes.[19]

Many Westerners equate jihad with terrorism. But not all jihadists are terrorists. As previously explained jihad means "struggle," and some jihadists carry on the struggle by means of stealth and subterfuge. That's why many American Muslim leaders seem "moderate" when they give English-language interviews and speeches, but when they speak to private gatherings in Arabic, they talk about subverting, sabotaging, and subjugating Western society.

Islamists call this kind of subterfuge *taqiyya*. This word means "religious dissimulation or deception." It's the practice of deceiving others and concealing one's true aims in order to achieve victory for Allah. The practice of taqiyya is especially emphasized in the Shia Islamic sect. Because the Shiites have so often been an oppressed minority, they developed taqiyya as a survival technique.

In Arabic, *taqiyya* literally means "caution." A related word is *kitman*, which means "concealment." Because of the widespread practice of taqiyya in the Islamic community, we can never know if a seemingly moderate Muslim is truly moderate—or simply advancing jihad by concealed means.

One example of the practice of taqiyya in our society involves the Boy Scouts of America. For years, the Islamic Society of North America (which has ties to the Muslim Brotherhood and Hamas) and the Islamic Council on Scouting of North America (ICSNA) have partnered with the Boy Scouts on interfaith events at the Boy Scouts National Jamboree.[20]

The chairman of ICSNA, Muzammil H. Siddiqi, has been widely viewed as a moderate Muslim. He was even invited by President George W. Bush to lead a prayer at the Interfaith Prayer Service at Washington National Cathedral a few days after 9/11.[21] But is Siddiqi genuinely moderate, or is he practicing taqiyya—religious deception—in order to conceal his true agenda?

Siddiqi tipped his hand in an October 18, 1996, newspaper column he wrote in *Pakistan Link*:

> It is true that Islam stands for the sovereignty of Allah subhanahu wa ta'ala and Allah's rules are not limited to the acts of worship, they also include social, economic and political matters. By participating in a non-Islamic system, one cannot rule by that which Allah has commanded. But things do not change overnight. Changes come through patience, wisdom and hard work.
>
> I believe that as Muslims we should participate in the system to safeguard our interest and try to bring gradual change for the right cause, the cause of truth and justice. We must not forget that Allah's rules have to be established in all lands, and all our efforts should lead to that direction.[22]

This statement by the chairman of the Islamic Council on Scouting of North America is a textbook example of taqiyya—Islamic religious deception. This is evidence that the Boy Scouts of America—an organization founded in 1910 to help instill patriotism and Christian values in American youth—has been infiltrated by a stealth-jihadist organization that intends to use the Boy Scouts as a means to incrementally impose "Allah's rules," Sharia law, on Western civilization.

Another form of stealth jihad is the Sharia finance industry—another missionary (dawah) arm of Islam. The goal of Islamic financiers is to infiltrate the Western financial sector and persuade Western investors to use Sharia-compliant investment practices. In this way, the Islamists can gain a toehold in our financial system with the ultimate goal of gaining control of the Western economy. Companies that engage in Sharia-compliant banking include Barclays, Citibank, Credit Agricole, Deutsche Bank, Goldman Sachs, HSBC Holdings, INVESCO Perpetual, Merrill Lynch, and Morgan Stanley.[23] A Sharia-compliant financial institution must tithe (zakat) a portion of its assets—and those tithes often end up funding jihad and terrorism.

Stealth jihad only works if we in the non-Muslim world give way to it and bow down to it. Islam only gains ground in the Christian West if we willingly surrender ground. One example of how we surrender without a struggle to stealth jihad is in our news reporting. Many in the news media simply agree to report the news from an "Islamically correct" point of view.

A prime example is the way news agencies report on events affecting the Temple Mount in Jerusalem. The Palestinian Authority currently governs parts of the West Bank and Gaza Strip, and hopes someday to completely eliminate the nation of Israel from Palestine. One strategy for delegitimizing and weakening Israel involves rewriting Israel's history. The Palestinian Authority claims, for example, that the Holocaust never happened, that the Jews never lived in the Holy Land during biblical times, and that there was never a Jewish temple on the Temple Mount in

Jerusalem. In fact, the Muslim authorities who control the Temple Mount have reportedly bulldozed archeological evidence of the old Jewish temple in a bid to erase the Jews' historical claim to their homeland.[24]

There has never been an Arab state in Palestine, yet history records there have been *three Jewish states* in Palestine. The first was established by Joshua after the exodus from Egypt. The second was established under Ezra and Nehemiah after the Babylonian exile. The third—the modern State of Israel— was declared in 1948. Yet American news organizations willingly fall in line with the Palestinian agenda. National Public Radio, the *New York Times*, and the Associated Press have all treated proven historical facts about the Temple Mount as if they were merely a matter of opinion.

NPR Jerusalem correspondent Mike Shuster once reported, "The Jews say that the Temple Mount was the site of two ancient temples in the Jewish tradition that had been destroyed at various stages in ancient Jewish history."[25] The existence of the two Jewish temples is not merely a matter of "Jewish tradition" or what "the Jews say." It's a matter of historical, archaeological fact. Distorting the facts and favoring one side over another is not good journalism. It's surrendering to stealth jihad.

When referring to the site of the two temples, reporters of the *New York Times* must write, "the Temple Mount, which Israel claims to have been the site of the First and Second Temples." And at the Associated Press, reporters must present both viewpoints as equally valid: "Jews believe the mosques sit on the ruins of the First and Second Jewish temples, and revere as their holiest site a nearby wall believed to have surrounded the sanctuaries. Muslims say nothing existed on the hill before the mosques." That "nearby wall" is none other than the Western Wall of the ancient Temple courtyard.[26]

By treating objective, historical fact as if it were mere subjective opinion, these news organizations have sided with the Palestinian propaganda machine—and they have handed a victory to the jihadists. Islamic extremists do not have to fight and die in a holy war in order to defeat us. They are waging a campaign of stealth jihad against us—and we are surrendering without a fight.

EIGHT

The Global Caliphate

E VER SINCE ISLAM BEGAN, its goal has been the founding of a world empire.

Islam experienced a phenomenal expansion under Umar ibn al-Khattab, the second caliph. Under Umar, Muslim armies swept through present-day Iraq and Iran, and on into Central Asia and the Punjab region of Pakistan and India. Within a hundred years after Muhammad's death, the Empire of Islam stretched, as someone once said, "from the Pyrenees to the Punjab, from the Sahara to Samarkand." This empire began to decline by the end of the tenth century.

Islam experienced a resurgence from the fifteenth to eighteenth centuries. It formed three powerful new empires—the Mughal in India, the Safavieh in Iran, and the expansionist Ottoman Empire in present-day Turkey. Islam spread into many new regions in Africa, Asia, and the Middle East, where millions converted to Islam, either voluntarily or at sword point. By the end of the sixteenth century, the Ottomans had conquered Greece, Bulgaria, and Turkey. Constantinople, long a bulwark of Christendom, fell in 1453 and became Istanbul, the Ottoman capital.

Many once-Christian regions became Muslim strong-holds. Forced conversions to Islam were commonplace. Sons of Christian parents were taken from their homes, reared as Muslims, and enrolled in the armies of Islam. Churches became mosques. The advance of Islam continued until 1529, when the Ottomans were stopped at the gates of Vienna.

That's ancient history, some would say. Yet many of the political problems and ethnic clashes we see today are rooted in the Muslim invasions of the seventh through sixteenth centuries. As we have seen, even today many Islamists call Westerners "Crusaders" (*al–Salibia*), because what is ancient history to us is yesterday's news to Muslims.

How Do Militant Muslims View Christianity?

Militant Islamists view Christianity as the foremost foe of Islam. Christianity blocks the advancement of Islam on virtually all geographic, historical, and ideological fronts. Islamists resent Christianity for four primary reasons.

First, Islamic militants see Christianity as the primary expression of infidel values and practices. Because the Islamists mistakenly assume that Christian values pervade Western civilization in the same way Islamic ideology pervades the Muslim world, they identify all of our culture's ills with Christianity. Muslims see Hollywood vice and violence as the result of Christian influence.

Second, because of the number of Christians in the world and the history of the Crusades, Islamic extremists see Christianity as the most potent ideological threat they face—far more potent than other religions, communism, or atheism. If Islam's most potent foe can be subjugated, then all other foes can easily be eliminated.

Third, though Muslims regard Christianity as a potent ideology, Muslim extremists regard Christians themselves as soft, passive targets. Muslims look at our Western tolerance and freedom, and they interpret it as a weakness they can exploit to subjugate us. America, following in the footsteps of Europe, has made a seemingly suicidal decision not to defend its culture from being infiltrated and undermined by Islamists—and they are busily taking advantage of our laxness.

Fourth, Islamic extremists see the Christian West, and especially the United States, as being responsible for many of the social ills people suffer in the Middle East—poverty, ignorance, unrest, and oppression. Above all, the Islamists blame the United States for the establishment and continued existence of the State of Israel. They also resent America for establishing US military bases in Saudi Arabia and other Muslim nations. And they blame America for corrupting Muslim culture with Western entertainment and attire.

Islam's "Holy War" Against Christianity

As a result of this growing resentment, Christians around the world have been targets of violence perpetrated by Muslim extremists. Some examples:

- Enraged Pakistani Muslims killed fifteen parishioners of a church in Behawalpur. The attack came shortly after American military troops entered Afghanistan in October 2001.[1] Though Pakistani Christians had nothing to do with American actions, to a Muslim extremist, a Crusader is a Crusader.

- Muslims have waged a twenty-year holy war against Christians in Sudan, resulting in more than two million deaths and thirteen million refugees. Sudanese clerics have issued a fatwa stating, "America is the greatest enemy of Islam and it embraces blasphemy, guards the Jews, and protects their terrorism."[2]

- In March 2012, Sheik Abdul Aziz bin Abdullah, the Grand Mufti of Saudi Arabia, called for the destruction of "all the churches of the region." The Grand Mufti is one of the most influential authorities in the Muslim world, yet his statement went unreported in the *New York Times*, *Washington Post*, and *USA Today*.[3]

- According to the Middle East Forum, the departure of US forces from Iraq has led to intense persecution of Iraqi Christians. The Forum's director, Raymond Ibrahim, said, "Half of Iraq's indigenous Christians are gone due to the unleashed forces of jihad."[4]

- The Arab Spring has forced many Egyptian Christians to flee persecution. Roughly one hundred thousand Coptic Christians have fled the country since the downfall of Hosni Mubarak and the rise of Islamic fundamentalist groups.[5]

Moderate Muslims point out the Koran actually blesses Christians and Jews: "Those who believe (in the [Koran]), and those who follow the Jewish (scriptures), and the Christians and the Sabians—any who believe in Allah and the Last Day, and work righteousness, shall have their reward with their Lord; on them shall be no fear, nor shall they grieve" (Koran 2:62).

At first glance, this verse seems to suggest that Islam considers Jews, Christians, and Sabaeans (an idol-worshipping people in the region now known as Yemen) to be blessed by Allah. But Muslim scholars generally interpret this verse as a blessing on the Christians and Jews who lived before Muhammad came and delivered the "complete revelation" of the Koran. Few Muslims would apply this blessing to Jews and Christians today.

Most of the verses of the Koran preach intolerance. The Koran tells Muslims, "Fight those who believe not in Allah nor the Last Day" (Koran 9:29), kill unbelievers who do not offer you peace—"slay them wherever ye catch them" (Koran 2:191, 4:91), and "take not the Jews and the Christians for your friends" (Koran 5:51). The Koran also says that Jews and Christians believe in superstition and false worship (Koran 4:51), that Allah will not forgive those who believe in the Trinity (Koran 4:48, 28:62–64), and that Christians—those who believe that Jesus is God—will burn in the fires of hell (Koran 5:72). The Koran says that Christians are perverse for believing that Jesus is the Son of God, and it invokes God's destruction on them (Koran 9:30; 19:35–37).

Muslims who wish to attack and persecute Christians can find support for their actions throughout the Koran.

Islam at War with Itself

Why do Muslims kill other Muslims? Much of the strife comes from the centuries-long conflict between Sunni Muslims and Shiite Muslims—a split that goes back to the early years of Islamic history.

Following the death of Muhammad, his friend Abu Bakr was named the first caliph. He was one of the first converts to Islam, and was Muhammad's close adviser in addition to being his father-in-law. The choice of Abu Bakr to lead the newly founded Islamic community—the *Ummah*—disappointed Ali ibn Abi Talib, Muhammad's kinsman and friend. Ali considered himself to be the true heir and successor of Muhammad, but he did not assume power until two other successors, the second and third caliphs, had died.

After Ali was named caliph, a power struggle ensued and Ali was assassinated during his prayers by Abd-al-Rahman ibn Muljam, who stabbed him with a poisoned dagger. After Ali's death, his eldest son Hasan ibn Ali claimed that, as Muhammad's grandson, he was next in line as successor to the caliphate. The struggle that followed split the Muslim empire into two factions. One group was the *Shi-at Ali* (the party of Ali), which supported the descendants of Ali as the rightful rulers of the Islamic world. These became known as the Shias or Shiites. The other group became the Sunnis (followers of the *sunna*, or path, of the Prophet Muhammad).

Hasan ibn Ali was later poisoned and his brother, Hussein ibn Ali, was beheaded at the Battle of Karbala. The Shiites still nurse a grudge against the Sunnis, feeling aggrieved over the death of Hussein more than thirteen centuries ago. As James Cook observed:

> They [the Shiites] became dissenters, subversives within the Arab empire, given to violence against authority. Shiite Islam was an extremely emotional sect and still is. Its adherents at times clothe themselves in black cloaks and black turbans, and once a year re-enact the passion of [Hussein], sometimes flagellating themselves as a means of atoning for [Hussein's] martyrdom.[6]

Shiites believe that the descendants of Ali are the *imams* (leaders). Imams are considered to be sinless and virtually infallible leaders in all spheres of life, including politics. Shiites believe in a continuing revelation of Allah through the imams. Therefore, the imams are the only ones capable of properly interpreting the Koran.

The Twelver Shiite sect teaches that the Twelfth Imam—Muhammad ibn Hasan al-Mahdi—went into hiding in the ninth century and will remain hidden until the Last Days, when he will be revealed as the Mahdi. He will emerge along with Isa (Jesus) to establish a global Caliphate and a golden age of peace and righteousness.

Twelver Shiites believe that until the Twelfth Imam returns, every true Muslim must place himself under the authority of an *ayatollah* (holy man). This belief has given rise to a strong clergy and a rigid religious hierarchy. Ayatollahs wield enormous power in Shiite culture.

Early in the sixteenth century, Twelver Shia Islam became the official religion of Persia (now called Iran). The clergy became increasingly powerful and developed a tradition of opposing the political state, claiming that the state owed religious obedience to the clergy. In 1906 the Shiite clergy in Persia led a revolution that established a constitution and caused the fall of the two-hundred-year-old Qajar dynasty. This gave rise to the first Pahlavi Shah, Reza Shah, and the fall of the second, Muhammad Shah.

In Iran, the Ayatollah Khomeini played on the Twelver Shiites' expectation of the return of the Twelfth Imam. Khomeini claimed to be a linear descendant of Ali and took the title of imam, encouraging his followers to believe that he might be the long-awaited Mahdi. After leading the successful ouster of Mohammad Reza Pahlavi, Shah of Iran, Khomeini reshaped Iran to conform to his ideology. Most importantly, he restructured the government so that the clergy would have absolute control.

Next, Khomeini worked to export his concept of theocratic government to other nations. He declared that Iraqi dictator Saddam Hussein was Muawiyah—the original antagonist of Ali from fourteen centuries ago, returned from the grave to kill Khomeini. Hussein, fearing that the Iranian Revolution would spread to his own country, attacked Iran in late 1980. Thus began an eight-year border war. Both nations paid a heavy financial and human toll for the conflict. The war killed or wounded as many as a million Iranians and three hundred thousand Iraqis, and cost each side an estimated five hundred billion dollars, devastating the economies of both nations.

The economic toll on Iraq may have prompted Saddam Hussein to invade Kuwait in August 1990—an attempt to seize Kuwait's vast oil wealth. A second motive for the invasion of Kuwait was the ancient rivalry between Shiites and Sunnis. Iraq has a predominantly Shiite population, and the leadership of oil-rich Saudi Arabia is Sunni. Once Kuwait fell, it seemed likely that Iraq might continue on into Saudi Arabia, igniting an open Shiite-Sunni war. That prospect is one of the principal reasons the United States defended Kuwait and invaded Iraq.

In this brief survey of Islamic history, one fact becomes clear: Almost since its inception, Islam has been at war with itself. Century after century, caliphs and imams and ayatollahs and warriors have battled and killed one another in order to prove themselves to be the purest, most zealous, most dogmatic Muslims of all.

A Sect within a Sect: Wahhabism

The particular brand of Islam espoused by Osama bin Laden and his al-Qaeda confederates is Wahhabism, an austere fundamentalist branch of Islam founded by Abd al-Wahhab (1703–1787). Though this branch of Islam was instrumental in creating the Saudi monarchy, the Wahhabist sect now seems intent on bringing down the Saudi monarchy.

Wahhabism fiercely opposes anything viewed as *bidaa* (modernity). This Arabic word expresses such intense disgust toward cultural compromise that it is usually spoken only as a muttered curse. The Wahhabis despise any social or technological change that appears to deviate from the fundamental teachings of the Koran. At various times, such innovations as the telephone, radio broadcasts, public education for women, and music have all been declared bidaa.

The Wahhabis also believe their faith should never yield any ground in any land that Islam has conquered. For this reason, Saudi Arabia donated heavily to the mujahideen fighters who battled the Soviets in Afghanistan. The Soviets had invaded Muslim land, and they had to be driven out and the land reclaimed for Islam.

The ferocity of Wahhabi fighters is legendary. An Arab historian in the eighteenth century wrote of the Wahhabis, "I have seen them hurl themselves on their enemies, utterly fearless of death, not caring how many fall, advancing rank after rank with only one desire—the defeat and annihilation of the enemy. They normally give no quarter, sparing neither boys nor old men."[7]

Wahhabis advocate strict punishments for violators of the Koran: Thieves have their left hand amputated. Adulterers are stoned to death. Murderers and sexual deviants are beheaded. Since King Abdul Aziz ibn Saud unified Saudi Arabia in 1932, the royal dynasty has had to balance the demands of modernization against the intolerant beliefs of the Wahhabis.

No one knows how many Muslims in Saudi Arabia adhere to Wahhabism. Estimates range from 10 percent to as high as 70 percent. At least ten of the 9/11 hijackers came from Saudi Arabia and very likely were Wahhabis.

In recent years, moderate Islamic governments around the Persian Gulf have faced increasing opposition and unrest within their populations. In response, some of these governments have become more radical in order to appease the extremists within their borders. The growing trend in Muslim countries has been toward Islamic fundamentalist ideology, regardless of which branch of Islam is advocated.

As a result, the world is becoming increasingly dangerous. Muslims of every sect are becoming radicalized and are infiltrating and challenging Western culture. Extreme Islam seeks to destroy our culture, our faith, and the nation of Israel.

NINE

All Roads Lead
to Israel

O N THE FIRST NIGHT of the so-called Arab Spring in Egypt, I sat in front of the cameras for three hours in a major cable network studio in Atlanta. I did my best to convince an inexperienced, young anchor that events in Egypt were not taking the country toward the kind of American-style democracy that he and his media colleagues made it out to be.

Drawing on my firsthand knowledge of Egypt, as well as academic training, I sought to give him and his viewers a clear picture of what would unfold. I warned that Islamists would soon sweep these well-meaning, young demonstrators under the Egyptian sand. I was not invited back to the network after that.

Those of us who have watched the Middle East for decades, with a clear-eyed understanding of Islamic culture and history, knew what the Arab Spring was all about. For years, militant Islamists have longed to destroy the Egyptian peace treaty with Israel. The militants saw Hosni Mubarak, then president of Egypt, as the chief guardian of that treaty.

Let's toss aside all illusions. Mubarak did not keep the peace treaty out of warm and fuzzy feelings toward Israel. And his predecessor, Anwar Sadat, didn't forge peace with Israel out of a deep fondness for the Jewish state. The peace between Israel and Egypt has been kept from 1978 to this day because of one thing: American dollars.

The Camp David Accords—which won Nobel Peace Prizes for Sadat and Israeli prime minister Menachem Begin in 1978, and for President Jimmy Carter in 2002—were based on billions of dollars in subsidies from American taxpayers to Israel and Egypt. Those subsidies are still being paid to both nations today. As a taxpayer, I would much rather pay for peace than for war—though it's possible that we are subsidizing a future Armageddon. According to the US State Department, Egypt receives $1.3 billion annually in military aid (which Egypt must use to purchase weaponry from American arms manufacturers), plus millions in economic assistance from the US Agency for International Development. A Cornell economist estimated in 2011 that US military aid makes up about a third of Egypt's military spending.[1] The United States also agreed to pay about $3 billion annually to Israel in grants and military aid.[2]

So the peace accords are as much about money as they are about peace. And there's nothing wrong with that. For more than three decades, American taxpayers have been able to purchase peace in the Middle East at a cost of a few tens of billions of dollars. Compared to the trillions spent on wars in Iraq and Afghanistan, that's a bargain. Unfortunately, the brokered peace between Israel and Egypt is fragile and could shatter at any time.

The uprisings that ousted President Mubarak were led by a small group of Egyptian students. The students wanted freedom and democracy in Egypt. But once Mubarak resigned, the Islamists came out of hiding and flexed their muscles, taking over the Arab Spring movement and steering it toward their own goals.

The US government didn't see this coming. The young cable news anchor who interviewed me didn't see this coming. Only those who truly understand the mind of the extreme Islamist knew what was coming and were not caught by surprise.

Extremists and terrorists have taken advantage of the political disarray in Egypt. Thousands of al-Qaeda jihadists have moved into the Sinai desert and are launching terror attacks into Israel, using the Sinai as a base. Writing in their Huffington Post blog, Daniel Wagner and Giorgio Cafiero of Country Risk Solutions observed: "Amidst the turmoil that has ensued throughout post-Mubarak Egypt, al-Qaeda has established a stronghold in the Sinai from where jihadists routinely target Egypt and Israel. . . . Since Israel's withdrawal from Egyptian territory in 1982, the Sinai has proven to be Egypt's most ungovernable territory."[3]

An Island in an Islamic Sea

Israel is surrounded by twenty-six predominantly Muslim nations: Mauritania, Morocco, Algeria, Tunisia, Libya, Egypt,

Sudan, Ethiopia, Eritrea, Djibouti, and Somalia in northern Africa; and Yemen, Oman, U.A.E. (United Arab Emirates), Saudi Arabia, Qatar, Bahrain, Kuwait, Jordan, Syria, Lebanon, and Iraq in the Middle East. Farther east are the Muslim nations of Iran, Afghanistan, and Pakistan. Turkey to the north is a predominantly Muslim country with an officially secular government—though Turkish prime minister Recep Tayyip Erdoğan seems to be pushing the nation toward an Islamic theocracy.

Israel is a small island of a mere eighty-five hundred square miles in a vast Islamic sea. Such a tiny nation could hardly threaten the oil-rich Muslim world. Little Israel should go completely unnoticed by the great Arab world— yet the exact opposite is true. To Muslims, Israel is the fly in the soup that cannot be ignored.

Jewish-American author and radio commentator Dennis Prager explained the problem simply and clearly in an online talk at his Prager University website. He said that when he did his graduate studies at Columbia University's School of International Affairs, his professors claimed that the Middle East conflict was the most complex problem imaginable. In reality, Prager said, the Middle East conflict is amazingly simple:

> In a nutshell, it is this: One side wants the other side dead.
>
> Israel wants to exist as a Jewish state and to live in peace. Israel also recognizes the right of Palestinians

to have their own state and to live in peace. The problem, however, is that most Palestinians and many other Muslims and Arabs do not recognize the right of the Jewish state of Israel to exist. . . .

If, tomorrow, Israel laid down its arms and announced, "We will fight no more," what would happen? And if the Arab countries around Israel laid down their arms and announced "We will fight no more," what would happen?

In the first case there would be an immediate destruction of the state of Israel and the mass murder of its Jewish population. In the second case, there would be peace the next day.[4]

That is the essence of the Middle East problem. That is why the Middle East conflict is simple to understand and seemingly impossible to solve. It is very hard to bargain with people who are bent on killing you. As Hassan Nasrallah, the head of Hezbollah, once said, "We are going to win because they [the Jews] love life and we love death."[5]

The Islamists view Israel as a constant reminder of Islam's humiliation. The Islamist view was expressed by Osama bin Laden in a statement aired on Al Jazeera a few weeks after the 9/11 attacks: "We cannot accept that Palestine will become Jewish. . . . I swear by God [Allah] the Great, America will never dream nor those who live in America will never taste security and safety unless we feel security and safety in our land and in Palestine."[6]

The Dream of a Jewish Homeland

When longtime White House correspondent Helen Thomas attended the White House Jewish Heritage Celebration on May 27, 2010, a reporter asked for her comments on Israel. "Tell them to get the hell out of Palestine," she said. "Remember, these people [the Palestinian Arabs] are occupied, and it's their land." Thomas then suggested the Jews could "go home to Poland or Germany and America and everywhere else."[7] But the Jewish homeland is not "Poland or Germany." Those lands are where the Holocaust took place.

The Jews refer to the Holocaust as the *Shoah* (Hebrew for "the catastrophe"). In Germany and in German-occupied territories, Jews were systematically rounded up, shipped to concentration camps, and murdered in a state-sponsored campaign of mass extermination. Of the nine million Jews living in Europe before the Holocaust, two-thirds were killed—more than a million Jewish children, two million Jewish women, and three million Jewish men. Many Jews who fled the Holocaust had to be smuggled into Palestine in order to circumvent British immigration restrictions.

After World War II, vast numbers of Jewish Holocaust survivors and refugees demanded a homeland in Palestine—and the newly revealed horrors of Dachau and Auschwitz tilted global public opinion in favor of the Zionist Jews.

The truth is that the Jewish homeland has always been Israel, the land God promised to Abraham and his descendants. In 1914, some eighty-five thousand Jews lived in Palestine, alongside some six thousand Arabs. At that time, Palestinian

Jews outnumbered Palestinian Arabs fourteen to one. This population figure is often overlooked when Westerners discuss the Jewish-Arab conflict in Israel. The land of Israel has *continuously* been the Jewish homeland from the time of Abraham through the centuries of the Diaspora (Dispersion) and right up to the present day. Since biblical times, far more Jews than Arabs have lived in Palestine, and this was true long before the establishment of the State of Israel. So it is only reasonable that the Jews should have a homeland of their own on the land they have continuously occupied since Old Testament times.

The need for a Jewish homeland was underscored by the periodic times of persecution Jews suffered as they were dispersed around the world. Zionist journalist Theodor Herzl wrote in 1895:

> The idea which I have developed in this pamphlet is a very old one: the restoration of the Jewish State.
>
> The earth resounds with outcries against the Jews, and these outcries have awakened the slumbering idea. . . .
>
> I am absolutely convinced that I am right—though I doubt whether I shall live to see myself proved to be so. Those who are the first to inaugurate this movement will scarcely live to see its glorious close. But the inauguration of it is enough to give them self-respect and the joy of freedom of soul. . . .
>
> The Jewish State is essential to the world; it will therefore be created. . . .

Am I before my time? Are the sufferings of the Jews not yet grave enough? We shall see. . . .

If the present generation is too dull to understand it rightly, a future, a finer, and a better generation will arise to understand it. The Jews wish for a State—they shall have it, and they shall earn it for themselves.[8]

Herzl was right—he did not live to see the Jewish State become a reality, but the Jews did earn for themselves a home-land in the Middle East. Herzl died in 1904, forty-four years before Israel was restored as a nation.

Within hours after Israel declared its independence in 1948, five nations—Egypt, Syria, Lebanon, Iraq, and Yemen—declared war on the new Jewish State. Saudi Arabia sent a military contingent under Egyptian command. Thus began Israel's yearlong war for survival.

The war concluded with the 1949 armistice agreement, which gave Egypt control of the Gaza area. The West Bank region of Samaria and Judea came under Jordanian super-vision. The remainder of the land was declared to belong to Israel. Jerusalem became a divided city—east Jerusalem was apportioned to the Arabs, west Jerusalem to the Jews. Jordan controlled the entire Old City of Jerusalem, including the Temple Mount and many of the most revered Christian sites. Israel was admitted as a member of the United Nations on May 11, 1949.

In May 1967, Egypt sent troops into the Sinai Peninsula, ordered United Nations troops out of the area, and formed a military alliance with Jordan. In June, forces from Syria, Jordan, and Egypt moved simultaneously against Israel. The invasion quickly collapsed, and the conflict became known as the Six Day War. After Israel successfully repulsed the attack, the cease-fire lines gave Israel control of the Golan Heights, the West Bank, Gaza, and the Sinai. Jerusalem was unified under Israeli control.

The government of Israel later annexed the Golan Heights (Syria had controlled the Golan Heights for nineteen years and had used the land to launch attacks into Israel's Galilee region). Israel also annexed east Jerusalem. The remaining areas were not annexed but were controlled by an Israeli occupation force to prevent further attacks.

In 1973, while most Jewish civilians and soldiers were at Yom Kippur services, Egypt and Syria launched simultaneous attacks against Israel. Egyptian tanks crossed the Suez. Syrian tanks rolled into the Golan. The Israel Defense Force (IDF) was initially caught off guard but ultimately repulsed the attack. Israeli forces in the south crossed the Suez Canal into Egypt. In the north, IDF forces advanced to within twenty miles of Damascus.

The Soviet Union under Leonid Brezhnev threatened to enter the war, raising the specter of World War III. A cease-fire was brokered that required Israel to withdraw to its 1967 borders, making no claim to the new territories it had taken in Egypt and Syria. Both Israeli and Arab forces suffered heavy casualties.

The Arab Perspective

The British role in creating the State of Israel and America's role in defending Israel left a deep scar in the Arab psyche. Many Arab Muslims believe to this day that the Christian West planted Israel in their midst to assert control over the Middle East. They see the existence of Israel as a new manifestation of the ancient Crusades.

Muslims call the non-Muslim world the House of War, and the existence of Israel on land that once belonged (in their view) to the House of Islam is no small matter. It strikes at the heart of Islamic ideology and Arab pride. That's why Muslims will not rest until the Jews either accept the Islamic religion or leave Palestine—one way or another.

The Palestine Liberation Organization (PLO) was founded to bring about the "liberation" of Palestine from Jewish control and place it under Arab rule. PLO headquarters were initially in Jordan, but Jordan expelled the PLO in 1970 and the organization moved to Lebanon. Yasir Arafat rose to prominence during the transition.

A summit meeting in Oslo, Norway, in 1993 produced the Oslo Accords—an agreement between Israeli Prime Minister Yitzak Rabin and the PLO's Yasser Arafat. The Accords created the Independent Palestinian Authority (IPA), which had jurisdiction over Gaza and Jericho, and in subsequent years, has received governmental authority over Ramallah, Bethlehem, and other areas. The PLO has demanded, and continues to demand, the whole of the West Bank, including those areas settled and farmed by Israelis. The PLO also demands the entire Old City of Jerusalem.

Jerusalem has been the international capital city of the Jewish people since King David gained control of the city around 1004 BC. Though Jerusalem is never mentioned by name in the Koran, the al-Aqsa Mosque, which stands on the Temple Mount in Jerusalem, is mentioned several times in the Hadiths. According to the Hadiths, Muhammad supposedly declared that the blessing for a Muslim who prays in the al-Aqsa mosque is multiplied hundreds of times over and that the al-Aqsa mosque was the second mosque established on earth.

The Koran states that Allah miraculously swept up Muhammad and took him on a journey by night from the al-Haram mosque in Mecca to the al-Aqsa mosque in Jerusalem (Koran 17:1). The journey ended with Muhammad ascending directly into heaven from the rock now located in the Dome of the Rock shrine.

The Dome of the Rock was completed by Abd al-Malik on the Temple Mount in Jerusalem in AD 692. It was the first great religious building complex in the history of Islam and marked the beginning of a new era. It was a declaration to the world that Islam was to be the supreme religion of the world.

Many Bible scholars believe that the Dome of the Rock stands on the site of Solomon's original temple. In order for the Antichrist to manifest himself in the temple of Jerusalem, would a new temple have to be constructed on the site of the Dome of the Rock? No one knows for sure. We only know that any action Israel might take to remove the Dome of the Rock or turn it into a Jewish temple would send shockwaves through the Muslim community.

For thousands of years, Israel has been the focus of conquests and crusades. It is the land where Abraham, Jesus, and Muhammad walked—and centuries later, their followers still compete for control of its historic lands, its magnificent city, and its holy Temple Mount.

The Burden of Damascus

Though we have been talking about the history of Israel, a word needs to be said about the Syrian capital of Damascus, northeast of Israel. Damascus may well be the oldest continuously inhabited city in existence. For thousands of years, it has been a leading center of culture and commerce in the Middle East. The city has long been a crossroads for caravans and a green oasis for nomadic shepherds. Today, it's a metropolis of more than 2.5 million people.

Damascus holds a unique place in prophetic Scripture. The city is mentioned as existing in the time of Abraham (Genesis 14:15). Other Old Testament passages speak of the great marketplaces and political might of Damascus—and the false gods that were worshipped there. In Acts 9, Saul the Pharisee was on the road to Damascus, intending to imprison the Christians in that city, when he was struck by a blinding vision of Jesus. Saul the Pharisee received Jesus as Lord and became a great missionary, the apostle Paul. An intriguing prophecy regarding Damascus is found in Isaiah and Jeremiah:

> A prophecy against Damascus:
> "See, Damascus will no longer be a city
>   but will become a heap of ruins. . . .
> In the evening, sudden terror!
>   Before the morning, they are gone!
> This is the portion of those who loot us,
>   the lot of those who plunder us. (Isaiah 17:1, 14)

> Damascus has become feeble,
>   she has turned to flee
>   and panic has gripped her;
> anguish and pain have seized her,
>   pain like that of a woman in labor.
> Why has the city of renown not been abandoned,
>   the town in which I delight?
> Surely, her young men will fall in the streets;
>   all her soldiers will be silenced in that day,"
>   declares the Lord Almighty.
> "I will set fire to the walls of Damascus;
>   it will consume the fortresses of Ben-Hadad."
> (Jeremiah 49:24–27)

The city of Damascus has been captured many times by many kingdoms—the Aramaeans, the Assyrians, the

Babylonians, the Greeks under Alexander the Great, the Romans, the forces of Caliph Umar, and the Ottomans, to name a few. Yet in all those years of siege and conquest, the city has never been destroyed and has never been left uninhabited. Why is this important? It means that the biblical prophecies against Damascus remain to be fulfilled. Stay tuned!

The ancient biblical prophecies against Damascus, the Syrian capital, suggest that God intends to hold Damascus accountable for its long history of violence against innocent people, and especially for Syria's attacks against Israel. As the Psalmist has said:

> See how your enemies growl,
>   how your foes rear their heads.
> With cunning they conspire against your people;
>   they plot against those you cherish.
> "Come," they say, "let us destroy them as a nation,
>   so that Israel's name is remembered no more."
> With one mind they plot together;
>   they form an alliance against you. (Psalm 83:2–5)

God is watching over His people, Israel—and He will judge the cities and nations that wish to do Israel harm. That includes the city of Damascus. In the King James Version, the prophecy of Isaiah 17:1 begins with these words: "The burden of Damascus." Truly, the city of Damascus bears a great burden of guilt for its long history of violence against Israel, as well as its own people. Someday, God's judgment will be carried out, and Damascus will cease to be a city.

As civil war rages across Syria and as Syrian leaders plot the destruction of Israel, it seems ever more likely that the fateful "burden of Damascus" will fall upon that city right before our eyes. God will not allow crimes against Israel to go unavenged. He once told Abraham, "I will bless those who bless you, and whoever curses you I will curse; and all peoples on earth will be blessed through you" (Genesis 12:3).

In the timeline of history and Bible prophecy, all roads lead to Israel.

TEN

The Spreading Wildfire

THE ULTIMATE GOAL of Islam has not changed in fourteen centuries: Conquer the world and eradicate all other religions. The Koran tells all Muslims:

> Fight those who believe not in Allah nor the Last Day, nor hold that forbidden which hath been forbidden by Allah and His Messenger, nor acknowledge the religion of Truth, (even if they are) of the People of the Book, until they pay the Jizya [religious tax] with willing submission, and feel themselves subdued.
>
> The Jews call 'Uzair [Ezra] a son of Allah, and the Christians call Christ the son of Allah. That is a saying from their mouth; (in this) they but imitate what the unbelievers of old used to say. Allah's curse be on them: how they are deluded away from the Truth! (Koran 9:29–30)

According to the Koran, Allah commands all Muslims to subjugate every rival religion, especially Judaism and Christianity. And when you subjugate a religion, you subjugate the people who practice that religion and the land they live on.

It's worth noting that in the early years of Islam—the first decade or so, when Muhammad lived in Mecca—the religion he taught was largely about an inner spiritual struggle to live a righteous life. During that time, Muhammad attracted only one hundred and fifty or so converts to his newly founded religion. But in AD 622, when Muhammad led his followers to the city of Medina (then known as Yathrib), his message changed to one of struggle against unbelievers. With his new, more warlike message, he suddenly attracted many new converts. The number of his followers swelled to around ten thousand. Suddenly, Muhammad had an army; and with that army, Muhammad set out to conquer the world. By the time of his death in 632, Muhammad had converted—largely by force—almost the entire Arabian Peninsula.

Some might say, "Well, doesn't Christianity seek world domination too? What about the Great Commission? Didn't Jesus send His followers out to conquer the world in His name?" No. Jesus did not command His followers to subjugate the world. He sent them out to preach the gospel and *invite* all people to receive Him as Lord and Savior. Jesus told them, "Go into all the world and preach the gospel to all creation. Whoever believes and is baptized will be saved, but whoever does not believe will be condemned" (Mark 16:15–16).

Genuine Christianity always invites. It never forces, never conquers. Those who freely accept the good news of Jesus by faith are saved and will live forever. Those who reject the good news will perish, but it is a choice they are free to make. Christians are commanded only to preach the gospel, never to impose it on the unwilling at the point of a sword. Christianity is spread by attraction and conversion. Islam is spread by conquest and subjugation.

Christianity's critics might say, "What about the Crusades? Weren't the Crusades an attempt to conquer and convert the world at the point of a sword?"

I don't defend the excesses and crimes committed by the Crusaders in the Middle Ages: the pillaging of towns, the desecration of mosques and temples, and the massacres of Jewish and Muslim men, women, and children. A number of Christian leaders loudly opposed the Crusades even as they were going on. For example, thirteenth-century Oxford philosopher and Franciscan friar Roger Bacon warned that the Crusades would actually damage the cause of Christ because "those who survive, together with their children, are more and more embittered against the Christian faith."[1] And Bacon was right.

But whenever people talk about the evils and excesses of the Crusades, an important part of the story is almost always left out: The Crusades were a reaction to more than four hundred years of Islamic jihad and conquest. By the time the Crusades were launched, Islam had already conquered half of Christendom and slaughtered hundreds of thousands of innocent Christians.

Muslim armies conquered cities that had been the cradles of the early Christian church, including Antioch, Damascus, and Jerusalem. The Muslims destroyed thousands of Christian churches or converted them into mosques. The armies of Islam conquered the Persian Empire, much of the Byzantine Empire, and all of Christian North Africa and Spain.

The Muslim onslaught obliterated the once-vital North African church, which had produced such influential church leaders as Cyprian of Carthage and Augustine of Hippo. As historian Robert Louis Wilken explained in *The First Thousand Years*:

> By the middle of the eighth century more than fifty percent of the Christian world had fallen under Muslim rule. . . . The successors of Muhammad planted a permanent political and religious rival to Christianity and made Christians a minority in lands that had been Christian for centuries. Four hundred years later, when the Crusaders arrived in the East, an Arab historian observed that they had entered "the lands of Islam."[2]

While I don't defend the excesses of the Crusades, we need to remember that the Crusaders entered the fray (originally, at least) not as aggressors but as defenders of a Christianity that was under siege by Muslim invaders. The Crusades were an attempt to turn back a four-century tide of Islamic jihad, aggression, expansion, and conquest.

The Goal of Islamic Conquest

The goal of Islamic conquest has remained unchanged year after year, century after century, right up to our own era. In 1979, after the Islamic revolutionaries seized power in Iran, their spiritual leader, the Ayatollah Khomeini, declared, "The governments of the world should know that Islam cannot be defeated. Islam will be victorious in all countries of the world, and Islam and the teachings of the Koran will prevail all over the world."[3] Khomeini only reiterated what Muslim leaders and holy men have voiced for centuries, and still voice today.

While the United States battled Islamic insurgents in Iraq, Jordanian militant Abu Musab al-Zarqawi, then-head of al-Qaeda in Iraq, released a statement explaining the aims of his terrorist organization: "We are not fighting to chase out the occupier or to save national unity and keep the borders outlined by the infidels intact. . . . We are fighting because it is a religious duty to do it, just as it is a duty to take the Sharia [Islamic law] to the government and create an Islamic state."[4]

While writing his 2005 Arabic-language book *Al-Zarqawi—Al-Qaeda's Second Generation*, Jordanian journalist Fouad Hussein conducted many hours of interviews with terror leader al-Zarqawi (who was killed by a US Air Force bomb strike in 2006). In those conversations, al-Zarqawi laid out a seven-stage master plan for taking over the world and transforming it into a global Islamic state.

According to al-Zarqawi's timetable, Islam would achieve "definitive victory"—a worldwide Caliphate—by 2020.[5]

It's naive to assume that Islam's goals of domination are limited to the Middle East. Islam seeks global domination. Muslims are the predominant power in Indonesia, the world's fourth most populous nation, and they are increasing in power in the Philippines. Both nations are economic powerhouses in Southeast Asia.

Islam's power is rapidly increasing across Europe. There are about 4.3 million Muslims in Germany, constituting more than 5 percent of the population, and that number is growing rapidly. Spain has a growing number of Muslims, as does Italy. In Rome, a new mosque was constructed at an estimated cost of twenty million dollars. France has the largest Muslim population, with well over three million. Muslims are the second-largest religious group in France (Roman Catholics are the largest, Protestants the third largest).

In the 1980s, Mirza Khizar Bakht, the secretary-general of the First Interest-Free Finance Consortium, Great Britain's Islamic bank, expressed his dream of establishing a Muslim shopping center in central London's Regent Street or in Knightsbridge. The aim of the center was to "unite the whole Muslim world in London."[6] If you go to London today, you can see that his dream has largely become a reality. Arab money and Arab influence are on full display on the streets of London.

The London-based Islamic Council of Europe spends large sums on propaganda and has built mosques in every major European city. The twenty-eight-hundred-square-foot Central Mosque in London can seat around five thousand worshippers and has a minaret that competes with the city's cathedrals on the city's skyline. Tablighi Jamaat, a fundamentalist Muslim missionary sect, pushed hard for the construction of a "super mosque" that would have seated ten thousand people—almost three times the seating capacity of St. Paul's Cathedral—but the plan was turned down. England has gone from having a single mosque in 1945 to having more than fifteen hundred mosques today. Mosques are symbols of Islamic power, and Muslims are building them worldwide at a rate unprecedented in history.

Muslims are currently winning fifty million people annually to their faith. They are on track to make Islam the world's largest religion.

Islamic Expansion in the United States

Islam has expanded with great fervor in the United States in the last century. In the decade of the 1970s alone, Islam grew by 400 percent in the United States. Today, the number of Muslims in America is estimated at 2.6 million, and that number is expected to more than double to 6.2 million by 2030.[7] The three main reasons for this rapid growth are increased immigration, high birth rate, and conversion.

First, since the ratification of the 1965 Immigration Act by President Lyndon Johnson, waves of Muslim immigrants have flooded the United States. Zaid Salim Shakir, cofounder of Zaytuna College in Berkeley, California, and the former

Muslim chaplain at Yale, has openly expressed his goal of seeing America come under the rule of Sharia law. He said, "Every Muslim who is honest would say, 'I would like to see America become a Muslim country.'" Muslims, he added, cannot accept the legitimacy of the American constitutional order because it goes "against the orders and ordainments of Allah."[8]

A second reason for Muslim expansion in the United States is high birth rates among Muslim immigrant families, especially those who come from the Middle East. Muslim parents are diligent in passing down the teachings of Islam to their children.

Large families and high birth rates have long been viewed as part of the Islamic plan for world domination, and Muslim leaders have made no secret of this plan. In 1974, Algerian leader Houari Boumedienne told the United Nations, "One day, millions of men will leave the Southern Hemisphere to go to the Northern Hemisphere. And they will not go there as friends. Because they will go there to conquer it. And they will conquer it with their sons. The wombs of our women will give us victory."[9]

A third reason for the expansion of Islam in the United States is that a significant number of African-Americans have converted to Islam since the 1960s. Muslim leaders see black America as ripe for conversion. The message espoused by militant black Muslims is much the same as the message preached by militant Arab Muslims: America must be subjugated.

In June 1991, an African-American convert to Islam, Siraj Wahhaj, became the first Muslim to offer the opening prayer in the US House of Representatives. He quoted the Koran and appealed to Allah to grant the lawmakers guidance, righteousness, and wisdom. A year later, Wahhaj addressed a Muslim conference in New Jersey where he sounded far less moderate. The goal of Muslims, he said, is to replace the Constitution with the Koran and the caliphate.

"If we were united and strong," he said, "we'd elect our own emir leader and give allegiance to him. . . . If six to eight million Muslims unite in America, the country will come to us." In 1995, the US attorney for New York listed Wahhaj as an unindicted coconspirator in the case of the blind sheik Omar Abdel Rahman in his trial for conspiracy to overthrow the US government.[10]

Overall, 60 to 90 percent of all converts to Islam in the United States are African-American—and 80 percent of those converts were raised in the Christian church. In 1994, an article published in *Christianity Today* predicted, "If the conversion rate continues unchanged, Islam could become the dominant religion in Black urban areas by the year 2020."[11]

Most black Muslims do not turn to Islam because they are attracted to its theology, laws, or history. Rather, they are attracted to Islam's offer of power for the powerless. In recent years, Islam has experienced a surge in popularity in our nation's prisons. Dr. Mark S. Hamm of the Department of Criminology at Indiana State University writes:

Most inmates are radicalized by other radical inmates, and not by outside influences. . . . Former rivals, like the Crips and Bloods, are joining forces under Islamic banners. Neo-Nazis are becoming Sunni Muslims. Meanwhile, there is growing conflict within inmate Islam as various factions of the faith compete for followers, thereby pitting the Nation of Islam against Sunnis, Sunnis against Shiites, and Prison Islam against them all. Moreover, radicalization is developed on a prison gang model.[12]

Black Muslims in the United States have only marginally integrated with the wider community of orthodox Islam. The American movement has taken the title of "World Community of Islam in the West." Historically, orthodox Islam did not recognize Black Muslim Americans, but that is changing as orthodox Muslims discover the benefits of joining forces with less orthodox groups in order to magnify their power and influence.

What Happens to Muslims Who Convert to Another Religion?

We in America are so accustomed to our religious freedom that we assume that such freedom is universally respected. But Islam does not respect or tolerate differences of belief. Islamic nations consider Christian missionary activity a crime; those who engage in Christian evangelism are punished as criminals.

Many Muslims who converted to Christianity in North Africa and the Middle East are languishing in prisons, convicted of "apostasy," a term Muslims use for the crime of forsaking Islam. Ismail al-Faruqi, who taught Islamic studies at Temple University, explained the reasoning behind these laws:

> To convert out of Islam means clearly to abandon its world order, which is the Islamic state. That is why Islamic law has treated people who have converted out of Islam as political traitors. . . . [The state] must deal with the traitors, when convicted after due process of law, either with banishment, life imprisonment, or capital punishment. The Islamic State is no exception to this. But Islamic political theory does allow converts from Islam to emigrate from the Islamic state, provided they do so before proclaiming their conversion, for the state does not keep its citizens within its boundaries by force. But once their conversion is proclaimed, they must be dealt with as traitors to the state.[13]

Apostasy—the act of forsaking what Muslims consider to be the one true religion—is punishable not only by imprisonment but often by death. Many Islamic governments maintain a pretense of tolerance and even have a "religious freedom" clause in their constitutions. However, "religious freedom" in those countries is interpreted as (for example) the right of a Christian or Jew to convert to Islam. It is never interpreted as the right of a Muslim to convert to another religion.

Results of Islamic Rule

We in the West need to remove our rose-colored glasses and recognize that when an Islamic government takes power, we invariably see three painful consequences.

First, people under Islamic rule lose their personal freedoms. Once Muslims gain political control, they eliminate personal freedoms, especially freedom of speech and freedom of association. They also eliminate all external signs of non-Muslim culture.

Immediately after the Taliban seized power in Afghanistan in 1996, the Islamist regime banned employment and education for women, music and "equipment that produces the joy of music," movies, videos, TVs, computers, dancing, wedding parties, statues and framed pictures, applause at sports events, kite flying, pool tables, chess games, card games, children's toys and dolls, fireworks, jewelry, wine, and much more. Women were required to cover themselves head to toe in shroud-like burkas. A woman had to stay in her home unless accompanied by a male relative. Men were required to wear beards that extended a minimum of the width of one's fist.[14]

The religious police in Afghanistan, who enforced Sharia law, were trained by radical Wahhabis in Saudi Arabia. A sign posted on the wall of the Taliban's police headquarters read, appropriately enough, "Throw Reason to the Dogs. It Stinks of Corruption."[15]

The soccer stadium in Kabul became an arena for public spectacles of punishment. Thieves had hands amputated in front of cheering crowds. Fornicators were flogged, and adulterers were stoned to death. Men accused of homosexual activity were partially buried in the ground, then a stone wall was pushed over on them by a bulldozer. These sadistic punishments, clearly the product of a diseased mind, were devised by Mullah Mohammad Omar, the supreme leader of the Taliban. (Mullah Omar was Afghanistan's de facto head of state from 1996 to late 2001, when he went into hiding, probably in Pakistan.)[16]

Personal freedom is practically unknown in Saudi Arabia, the holy land of Islam. Like the Taliban, the Saudi government carries out Sharia law with floggings, amputations of hands and feet, stonings, beheadings with a sword, and even crucifixions.[17] Suhaila Hammad, the spokeswoman for Saudi Arabia's National Society for Human Rights, defended the practice of beheading condemned prisoners, saying, "Allah, our creator, knows best what's good for his people."[18]

Women's rights are almost nonexistent in Saudi Arabia. Women comprise only 5 percent of the Saudi workforce, the lowest percentage of any nation in the world.[19] It is against the law for women to drive cars in Saudi Arabia. (An odd loophole in the law permits women to pilot airplanes, but they must be driven to the airport by a man.)[20]

The Islamic tradition called *purdah* requires a complete separation between the sexes. The world of men and the world of women must never come in contact in Saudi society. Both men and women are required to cover most of their bodies, and Saudi women can never be seen in the company of a man who is not either her husband or a kinsman by *mahram*. A mahram relative is related either by blood (parent, grand-parent, sibling, uncle, aunt) or related by marriage (parent-in-law or stepparent), and thus unmarriageable.

There is an odd provision by which a man who is not related to a woman can become mahram through what is called "milk kinship." A woman must provide five meals of breast milk to the man in order to create this "kinship." For example, an aunt might provide five meals of breast milk to a young nephew-by-marriage so that the families can freely mingle when the nephew becomes a man. Though this custom seems grotesque to Western sensibilities, Islamic clerics take the matter seriously and debate such issues as whether a man should drink the milk from a bowl or straight from the woman's breast.[21]

Saudis do not grant basic human rights to non-Muslim visitors to their country, including American servicemen defending the Saudi Kingdom. The Saudis were pleased to accept help from the US military when Iraqi forces threatened to invade. But the Saudis imposed stifling restrictions on the four hundred thousand American soldiers during Operation Desert Shield. Soldiers could celebrate their religious holidays only in remote areas where the local citizens could not observe them. Christian and Jewish chaplains were forbidden to wear religious symbols in public (such as the Jewish *kippah* head covering or a Christian cross). There are no churches or synagogues in Saudi Arabia.

The second result of Islamic rule is that modernization and technological advances come to a grinding halt.

Apart from the oil-producing nations, most Islamic nations are poor. Wealth in the modern world has been strongly linked to modernization, and Islam stands against innovation, creativity, and progress. There's a saying attributed to Muhammad (though it is not in the Koran): "The worst things are those that are novelties. Every novelty is an innovation, every innovation is an error, and every error leads to Hellfire."[22]

Enough innovation has trickled into the Islamic world to show poor Muslims that they do not have the conveniences and material prosperity of the West. Muslims know they are missing out on many of the advancements of the modern world. This only aggravates their anger toward the West. They feel a paradoxical mixture of jealousy for the innovations we enjoy, mingled with a rejection of the "heresy" of all ideas and inventions that depart from the simple, impoverished "purity" of seventh-century Islam.

The message of the Islamists to poor Muslims is never outright denunciation of luxuries or technology. Rather, they say, "The reason you live in poverty is that America, the Great Satan, is doing this to you. Israel is doing this to you. Join our holy war. Join the army of Allah to defeat the West and end this oppression."

Islamic governments tend to be autocratic regimes in which the rich get richer and the poor get poorer. Economic mismanagement and corruption are widespread. A comment by an Algerian interviewed in a French news magazine is typical of opinions held throughout the Muslim world: "Algeria was once the granary of Rome, and now it has to import cereals to make bread. It is a land of flocks and gardens, and it imports meat and fruit. It is rich in oil and gas, and it has a foreign debt of twenty-five billion dollars and two million unemployed."[23]

The third painful consequence we see when Islamists take power is that bureaucratic governments fear the wrath of radical Muslims. In order to maintain their popularity and power, these governments often appease the hard-liners and zealots in their society. This is one reason you almost never hear moderate Muslims speak out against Muslim terrorists. To speak out is to incur the wrath of the extremists—so they keep silent. They appease the extremists to avoid trouble.

Appeasement is the policy of most Middle East governments. Here's an example of how a policy of appeasement works to placate radical factions.

Years ago, an Egyptian church was seized by radical Muslims in the town of El Basateen, near Cairo. The Muslims converted the building into a mosque. When Christians complained to the authorities that their property had been unlawfully taken, police demolished the building on the pretext that the Christians had not acquired the proper construction permits. Rather than confront the actions of the Muslim militants, the government adopted a hide-behind-the-law approach that caused even greater injustice for the Christians. This happens again and again in Middle Eastern societies.

Egyptian law states that no church may be built or have any alterations, repairs, or improvements without a presidential decree. This law was enacted in 1856 in accordance with the Covenant of Umar, a statute enacted when Egypt was an Ottoman colony.

In 1972, President Anwar Sadat promised Coptic Christian leaders he would grant fifty permits a year for church building. However, during the six years from 1973 to 1979, he granted a total of fifty permits, not the three hundred promised permits. By 1990, hundreds of applications were gathering dust in government offices. Some churches had waited for decades to obtain a building permit, even while the government was building mosques almost daily and paying the salaries of mosque leaders. After President Mubarak came to power, he reactivated and tightened the 1856 law, making it virtually impossible for new churches to be built or for old churches to be renovated.

Here is the irony: The policy of appeasing the hard-liners didn't help either leader. The hardliners assassinated Sadat and deposed Mubarak. Appeasing extremists never earns their gratitude—only their contempt. Appeasement always emboldens the oppressor.

Since 1973, Egypt has engaged in a continual effort to appease radical Muslims by passing laws paving the way for the Koran to be used as the primary source of law in Egypt. Court decisions have set precedents that push non-Muslims (including Coptic Christians) more and more into the role of *dhimmi*—non-Muslims whose rights are extremely limited under Sharia law.

In Saudi Arabia (which many in the West mistakenly view as a "moderate" Arab state), non-Muslims cannot be citizens, and non-Muslim tourists are treated with suspicion. The official website of Saudi Arabian Airlines (or Saudia, which is owned and operated by the Saudi government) has a page that lists items that tourists may not bring into the Kingdom of Saudi Arabia. As Middle East expert Daniel Pipes has noted, that page has disappeared from the Saudia website when the news media focus their attention on it. Items that are "not allowed" according to the official web site include "Bibles, crucifixes, statues, carvings, items with religious symbols such as the Star of David, and others." In short, you must respect the Islamic faith while the Saudis forbid you to even read your Bible as a "guest" of the kingdom.[24] This is perplexing, because the Koran admonishes all Muslims to read the Gospels (Koran 3:3, 84; 5:46).

Throwing Off the Yoke

After Egyptian prime minister Hosni Mubarak was deposed amid the Arab Spring uprisings, the nation held an election in June 2012. The people chose Mohamed Morsi, a leader of the Muslim Brotherhood, as Egypt's first democratically elected leader. But what do you do when a democratically elected leader decides to rule as a dictator?

Upon taking power, Morsi granted himself unlimited executive power. He claimed the power to write laws without being subject to judicial review. He issued a new constitution that was backed by the Islamist hard-liners. Journalists and dissidents were arrested under his rule.

The Egyptian people realized they had made a mistake. Month by month, unrest spread across the twenty-seven governorates of Egypt. A grassroots youth organization called Tamarod ("rebellion") collected millions of signatures on a petition calling for Morsi to resign. A nationwide protest was scheduled for June 30, 2013, exactly one year into Morsi's presidency.

The day of protest began with anti-Morsi marches across Cairo. Demonstrators filled Tahrir Square and overflowed into the city's streets, alleys, and parks. Crowds gathered in front of Morsi's mansion, waving Egyptian flags and red cards, demanding his resignation.

The demonstrators were not just angry with Morsi and the Muslim Brotherhood. They also expressed rage toward the US government, which had backed the Muslim Brotherhood in Egypt before Morsi's election and throughout his dictatorial reign. In fact, the US government had even tried to thwart the June 30 protests—and the Egyptian people were furious.

Reporter Sharif Abdel Kouddous was in Cairo during the protests. On the *Democracy Now!* program, which airs on NPR, PBS, Pacifica, and other stations, Kouddous said, "I've never seen the level of anti-Americanism and xenophobia in Egypt as in the past few weeks. . . . If you go to Tahrir, you see the pictures of Obama, you know, with like a beard and a turban, as if he's Osama bin Laden, and pictures of . . . [US Ambassador to Egypt Anne Patterson] with her face crossed out. . . . They see this as . . . [the US government] having backed Mohamed Morsi and the Muslim Brotherhood, and not spoken out despite repeated transgressions and repeated protests and repeated police abuse over the past year."[25]

The rage of the demonstrators is well founded. The US government has strongly supported Morsi and the Muslim Brotherhood, even though it was clear that Morsi was acting as a dictator and was actually siding with terrorists against the United States (for example, Morsi called for the United States to release "the blind sheikh," Omar Abdel-Rahman, who was implicated in the 1993 World Trade Center bombing, the 1981 assassination of Egyptian leader Anwar Sadat, and other terror plots).[26]

In cities across Egypt, demonstrators marched, chanted, formed human chains, and voiced their defiance of the Morsi regime and the Muslim Brotherhood. "National unity against the Muslim Brotherhood," chanted some protestors, while others shouted, "You who rule in the name of religion, where is justice and where is religion?"[27]

On Monday, July 1, 2013, Egyptian defense minister Abdel-Fattah el-Sissi delivered a statement on Egyptian TV. The statement, aimed at the Morsi regime, was part pleading, part warning: The government had forty-eight hours to respond to the demands of the people and hold a fresh election. The people had suffered enough, and national security was at risk. El-Sissi concluded, "If the demands of the people are not met within that time period, then we will be obliged to fulfill our historical duty towards our country and the great people of Egypt to map out a future plan for the country."[28]

The protests continued day and night until the evening of July 3, when the forty-eight-hour time limit expired. Defense Minister el-Sissi again went on live television—this time to inform the nation that Mohamed Morsi had been deposed. He had been hounded out of office by many of the same people who had voted for him a year earlier. Interviewed on CNN, retired Egyptian major general Sameh Seif Elyazal said, "We haven't seen . . . in modern history, any country in the world driving 33 million people in the street for four days asking the president for an early presidential election."[29] The people of Egypt had learned what it was like to be ruled by the Muslim Brotherhood—and they soundly rejected it.

Muslims threw off the yoke of political Islamism. Here is historic proof that there truly are moderate Muslims. Many Muslims look at the more extreme and violent passages of the Koran and say, "Well, those ideas may have been true at the founding of the religion, but they are not needed today. We do not need to be ruled by zealots and despots. We are Muslims, but we are not Islamists."

Those moderate Muslims have been silent. They have allowed the extremists in the Muslim Brotherhood, al-Qaeda, and ISIS to control the message. The extremists are probably no more than 20 percent or so of the Muslim world, but the 80 percent have been silent for too long. The uprising in Egypt, June 30, 2013, may well be the first time in history that Muslims have taken to the streets to protest Islamist rule.

These courageous Muslim citizens raised their voices as one and said "No!" to political Islam—and the rejection of political Islam in Egypt is emboldening others in Libya, Tunisia, and other Islamic countries to stand up to their oppressors. These are people we can reason with and dialogue with. These are even people we can reach with the gospel.

ELEVEN

A Spiritual Battle

DANIEL 10 RECORDS a prophetic vision that the prophet Daniel experienced after the Jews had begun returning home to Israel from their exile in Babylon. In this vision, God gave Daniel (and us) a glimpse of the spiritual realm where invisible spiritual forces press the buttons and pull the levers of human history. Daniel opens this section with these words:

> In the third year of Cyrus king of Persia, a revelation was given to Daniel (who was called Belteshazzar). Its message was true and it concerned a great war. The understanding of the message came to him in a vision. (Daniel 10:1)

Daniel tells us that he has received a message from God about a great conflict—a spiritual conflict. He continues:

> At that time I, Daniel, mourned for three weeks. I ate no choice food; no meat or wine touched my lips; and I used no lotions at all until the three weeks were over.

On the twenty-fourth day of the first month, as I was standing on the bank of the great river, the Tigris, I looked up and there before me was a man dressed in linen, with a belt of fine gold from Uphaz around his waist. His body was like topaz, his face like lightning, his eyes like flaming torches, his arms and legs like the gleam of burnished bronze, and his voice like the sound of a multitude.

I, Daniel, was the only one who saw the vision; those who were with me did not see it, but such terror overwhelmed them that they fled and hid themselves. So I was left alone, gazing at this great vision; I had no strength left, my face turned deathly pale and I was helpless. Then I heard him speaking, and as I listened to him, I fell into a deep sleep, my face to the ground.

A hand touched me and set me trembling on my hands and knees. He said, "Daniel, you who are highly esteemed, consider carefully the words I am about to speak to you, and stand up, for I have now been sent to you." And when he said this to me, I stood up trembling.

Then he continued, "Do not be afraid, Daniel. Since the first day that you set your mind to gain understanding and to humble yourself before your God, your words were heard, and I have come in response to them. But the prince of the Persian kingdom resisted me twenty-one days. Then Michael, one of the chief princes, came to help me, because I was detained there with the king of Persia. Now I have come to explain to you what will happen to your people in the future, for the vision concerns a time yet to come." (Daniel 10:2–14)

If you have ever wondered why evil seems to reign in the affairs of nations, here's the reason: Unseen rulers wage war against God. These spiritual rulers use men and nations as their proxies to carry on this hidden struggle. As the apostle Paul reminds us, "For our struggle is not against flesh and blood, but against the rulers, against the authorities, against the powers of this dark world and against the spiritual forces of evil in the heavenly realms" (Ephesians 6:12).

As this vision begins, Daniel stands beside the Tigris River, and there are others nearby. Daniel has prayed and fasted for three weeks. A man appears before Daniel, and he is dressed in white linen, with a golden belt encircling his waist. The man's face shines brightly and his eyes glow like fire. When he speaks, his voice is like many voices speaking at once. Who is this man?

The last book of the Bible gives us a clue. In Revelation 1:13–16, John has a vision of Jesus Christ. The Lord is dressed in a robe bound with a golden belt, with a face that shines like the sun and eyes that glow like fire. His voice sounds like rushing waters. The parallels between the visions of Daniel and John are no coincidence. Both prophets were given a glimpse into the invisible battle being waged by the rulers of the spiritual realm. I believe Daniel and John saw the same Man—and this means that Daniel probably experienced a "theophany," an Old Testament manifestation of the pre-incarnate Christ.

Only Daniel could see this man. But Daniel's vision touched off such an intense spiritual shockwave that all the people around him fled in fear. Daniel, too, was afraid, so that his hands and knees trembled uncontrollably. The man touched Daniel and said, "Do not be afraid, Daniel. Since the first day that you set your mind to gain understanding and to humble yourself before your God, your words were heard, and I have come in response to them. But the prince of the Persian kingdom resisted me twenty-one days."

Notice that number: twenty-one days. Earlier, in verse 2, Daniel said he had fasted, prayed, and mourned "for three weeks"—or twenty-one days. This miraculous man is telling Daniel that *at the exact moment that Daniel began to fast and pray*, God sent the answer to his prayer.

Why did it take three weeks for God's answer to arrive? "The prince of the Persian kingdom," the man said, "resisted me twenty-one days." The "prince of the Persian kingdom" was not a human prince but a demonic prince. The man adds, "Then Michael, one of the chief princes, came to help me, because I was detained there with the king of Persia." This spiritual battle lasted twenty-one days—but then Michael, "one of the chief princes," came to the aid of this messenger.

This is the first time in Scripture that the archangel Michael is mentioned. He appears again in Daniel 10:21

and 12:1, Jude 1:9, and Revelation 12:7. Michael is one of the mightiest angels, and he is the prince of the people of Israel—a righteous prince and an angelic servant of God. In the invisible spiritual realm, nations have spiritual "princes" ruling over them. Righteous nations, like Israel, have a righteous prince. Pagan nations, like Persia, are oppressed by an evil prince—a demon. Though demons are fierce and powerful, they are no match for the angels of the Lord. We need not fear the demons, even if they cause the economy to collapse, the society to crumble, and the machines of war to roar all around us. The Lord has said:

> You will not fear the terror of night,
> nor the arrow that flies by day . . .
> For he will command his angels concerning you
> to guard you in all your ways. (Psalm 91:5, 11)

The next time you think God is delaying in answering your prayers, remember the example of Daniel, who fasted and prayed for three weeks. God instantly began to answer Daniel's prayer—but sometimes God needs to work out all the circumstances for our prayers to be answered. In Daniel's case, God had to deal with the "prince of the Persian kingdom" (Daniel 10:13). The *human* ruler of Persia at that time was Cyrus, the king who had issued the decree allowing the Jews to return to Israel. Perhaps God had to wage spiritual warfare with the demonic "prince" of Persia for control of the heart and mind of King Cyrus.

From a human perspective, it often seems that God delays in answering our prayers. The seeming delays occur because we live in a fallen world—a spiritual battlefield where the forces of God and the forces of Satan wage continual war. Demons oppose God's work, and many of those demons are assigned to the nations of the earth. Once we recognize that we are engaged in a cosmic struggle "against the powers of this dark world and against the spiritual forces of evil in the heavenly realms" (Ephesians 6:12), many of the confusing events in this world—including the struggle between Christianity and Islam—come into sharp focus.

The next time you watch the news about events in the Middle East, remember Daniel's vision. Remember that the spiritual forces of evil are constantly striving against God. These evil forces cannot defeat our God, but they can cause destruction and delays. They can inflict many human casualties. But you don't have to be a casualty of that cosmic spiritual struggle. You can be victorious over "the spiritual forces of evil in the heavenly realms."

The Parable of the Fig Tree

As the spiritual battle rages and the world grows darker and more evil, Jesus says, don't be anxious or upset. Rejoice! The redemption of your body is at hand. The kingdom of God is near.

In His discourse on the Mount of Olives, Jesus tells His disciples:

Now learn this lesson from the fig tree: As soon as its twigs get tender and its leaves come out, you know that summer is near. Even so, when you see all these things, you know that it is near, right at the door. Truly I tell you, this generation will certainly not pass away until all these things have happened. Heaven and earth will pass away, but my words will never pass away. (Matthew 24:32–35)

Luke also records the lesson of the fig tree that Jesus spoke of, and Luke's account reveals some additional insights:

"When these things begin to take place, stand up and lift up your heads, because your redemption is drawing near." He told them this parable: "Look at the fig tree and all the trees. When they sprout leaves, you can see for yourselves and know that summer is near. Even so, when you see these things happening, you know that the kingdom of God is near." (Luke 21:28–31)

Now, we as believers in Christ have already been redeemed from sin and judgment. So what did Jesus mean when He said, "When these things begin to take place, stand up and lift up your heads, because your redemption is drawing near"? He was talking about *the redemption of the body*. We are already spiritually redeemed, but when Jesus returns for us, we will be physically redeemed as well. As the apostle Paul explains, "Not only so, but we ourselves, who have the firstfruits of the

Spirit, groan inwardly as we wait eagerly for our adoption to sonship, the redemption of our bodies" (Romans 8:23).

Some people are baffled by the Lord's parable of the fig tree, but I don't think His words are difficult to understand. The fig tree is common in Israel. Jesus is saying that everyone knows the life cycle of the fig tree. In the springtime, when the green twigs and leaves begin to bud on the fig tree, people know that summer, the time of harvest, is just a few months away.

In the Old Testament, the harvest is a metaphor for God's judgment. In the Scriptures, the time of judgment is a time of separation—the separation of the wheat from the chaff, the sheep from the goats, the believers from the nonbelievers. Jesus wants us to know that when we see certain signs of the times, we know that the summer of harvest is coming soon. The apostle Paul tells us how we should respond when we realize the summer of harvest is approaching:

And do this, understanding the present time: The hour has already come for you to wake up from your slumber, because our salvation is nearer now than when we first believed. The night is nearly over; the day is almost here. So let us put aside the deeds of darkness and put on the armor of light. (Romans 13:11–12)

What, then, are the signs Jesus tells us to look for?

Signs of the Times

In His Olivet Discourse, Jesus describes a number of signs leading up to the end times.

First, in Matthew 24:4–8, there are the signs of "the beginning of birth pains" that precede the end times: False teachers. Wars and rumors of wars. Famines and earthquakes.

Second, in verses 9–14, we see an intensifying of the signs, and we know that the end times are fast approaching. Christians will be hated and persecuted. Many who profess to be Christians will turn false and defect from the faith. False prophets will deceive many. Wickedness will increase; most people will become evil, selfish, and unloving. At the same time, the gospel will be preached as a witness to all nations.

Third, in verses 15–28, the Antichrist sets up "the abomination that causes desolation" in the holy place of the temple. The Lord's tone is urgent: "Then let those who are in Judea flee to the mountains. Let no one on the housetop go down to take anything out of the house. Let no one in the field go back to get their cloak" (vv. 16–18). The horrors of the Great Tribulation will increase as the end times reach their climax.

Fourth, in verse 29, the sun and moon darken, the stars fall from the sky, and the planets are shaken in their orbits. It is a time of cosmic chaos—yet Jesus says His people must not cringe in fear. They should rejoice, because their day of redemption is near.

Fifth, in verses 30–31, the Lord returns in power and glory to bring history to a close—and Jesus makes a fascinating statement: "Truly I tell you, this generation will certainly not pass away until all these things have happened" (v. 34). In this context, it's obvious Jesus is saying the generation that witnesses these cosmic catastrophes will also witness the return of Christ.

Many have wrenched that verse out of context and quote it as a "failed prediction" that Jesus would return in the lifetime of His hearers. In context, it's clear that Jesus was speaking of a *future* generation—the generation that witnesses all the signs He lists in the preceding verses.

For unbelievers, the end times will be an experience of magnified terror. But for those who know the Lord Jesus and place their trust in Him, it will be a time of rejoicing and deliverance. When that day comes, will you regret the missed opportunities of your life? Or will you rejoice that Jesus has come to put an end to sin, suffering, and sorrow?

The Coming Judgment

Some in the church today claim Jesus didn't come to save us from hell, nor did He come to bring us eternal life. Some even make the ridiculous claim that Jesus never spoke about hell, even though most of what we know about hell and judgment came from the lips of Jesus Himself.

When Jesus offers "eternal life," He is not merely promising some transcendent quality of life. He is promising resurrection, He is promising life after death, and He is promising eternity in heaven instead of hell.

Jesus said, "Very truly I tell you, whoever hears my word and believes him who sent me has eternal life and will not be judged but has crossed over from death to life" (John 5:24). And, "For my Father's will is that everyone who looks to the Son and believes in him shall have eternal life, and I will raise them up at the last day" (John 6:40). Statements such as these leave no room for reinterpretation.

The Lord spoke often of judgment and hell—yet He always spoke in the most caring and compassionate language. He understood the horrors of hell, and that is why He pleaded with people to repent and accept God's plan of salvation.

Though Jesus spoke of the coming judgment, He never did so in a spirit of hostility. Instead, He demonstrated compassion and empathy. He wept over Jerusalem, knowing the city would soon reject Him and crucify Him, just as it had killed the prophets who came before Him. Jesus is not willing that any should perish, but He will not force His salvation on anyone who chooses rebellion instead.

Unbelievers and false teachers think it is cruel and unfair for God to judge sinners. But we who are saved don't marvel that God judges sin. We marvel that God offers us forgiveness! Though we are worthy of judgment, Jesus redeemed us from sin.

When will the final judgment begin? It will begin when Jesus appears. Immediately after the sun and moon darken and the stars fall, as the unbelievers wail and die of fright, Jesus will come in power and glory—and in judgment. In the Olivet Discourse, Jesus describes the judgment of the ungodly when He says, "Depart from me, you who are cursed, into the eternal fire prepared for the devil and his angels" (Matthew 25:41).

In Revelation, John describes the judgment this way:

> Then I saw a great white throne and him who was seated on it. The earth and the heavens fled from his presence, and there was no place for them. And I saw the dead, great and small, standing before the throne, and books were opened. Another book was opened, which is the book of life. The dead were judged according to what they had done as recorded in the books. The sea gave up the dead that were in it, and death and Hades gave up the dead that were in them, and each person was judged according to what they had done. Then death and Hades were thrown into the lake of fire. The lake of fire is the second death. Anyone whose name was not found written in the book of life was thrown into the lake of fire. (Revelation 20:11–15)

Judgment holds no terror for those whose names are written in the book of life. But those whose names are not in the book will have no way of escape.

Rising Persecution

The Lord could return this instant, or He might delay His return for thousands of years. Throughout history, many people have mistakenly predicted an early date for His return.

Ignatius of Antioch lived from about AD 35 to 107 and was discipled by the apostle John. Ignatius once wrote, "The last days are upon us. Weigh carefully the times. Look for Him who is above all time, eternal and invisible."[1] Though his prophetic timing was off, Ignatius offered excellent counsel—look for Jesus and always be ready for His return.

Hippolytus of Rome (170–235) calculated that Christ was born fifty-five hundred years after the creation of Adam, and he decided that Christ's return would occur six thousand years after Adam, in AD 500. He also concluded that the Antichrist was probably one of the Roman emperors, such as Nero or Domitian.[2] Hippolytus demonstrates the futility of trying to set a date for the end times based on a series of assumptions and mathematical calculations.

Christopher Columbus was convinced that the world would end in 1656. In 1492, he sailed westward to find a short-cut to India, unaware that North and South America blocked his path. He believed that by taking Christianity to India, he would hasten the return of Jesus Christ—and the end times. In 1500, he wrote a letter to the royal court of Spain, saying, "God made me the messenger of the new heaven and the new earth of which he spoke in the Apocalypse of St. John."[3] He was as mistaken about the end times as he was about a shortcut to India.

We mustn't be presumptuous about setting dates and times. In humility, we must accept the Lord's statement: "But about that day or hour no one knows, not even the angels in heaven, nor the Son, but only the Father" (Matthew 24:36). Yet Jesus has revealed to us a number of signs.

We know we are already experiencing "the beginning of birth pains" that precede the end times: false teachers, wars, rumors of wars, famines, and earthquakes. Even more significantly, we are seeing an intensifying of the next set of signs of the approaching end times: a rise in hostility toward Christians.

A 2014 Pew Research report found that Christians are the world's most oppressed religious group, with persecution especially intense in North Korea and the Muslim world. In fact, the Pew study shows that religious hostilities dramatically increased during the Arab Spring.[4]

But Christianity is under fire not only in communist and Islamic nations—Christians are also under attack in America. Kelly Shackelford, founder of the Liberty Institute, says the government is increasingly trying to silence Christians in America. "I have been doing these types of cases for almost twenty-five years now," Shackelford said. "I have never seen the levels of attacks like these and how quickly they are now proliferating." A joint report by the Liberty Institute and the Family Research Council cited many examples, including:

- A public school official physically lifted an elementary school student from his seat and reprimanded him in front of his classmates for praying over his lunch.
- A public school official prevented a student from handing out flyers inviting her classmates to an event at her church.

- A public university's law school banned a Christian organization because it required its officers to adhere to a statement of faith that the university disagreed with.

- The US Department of Justice argued before the Supreme Court that the federal government can tell churches and synagogues which pastors and rabbis it can hire and fire.

- The State of Texas sought to approve and regulate what religious seminaries can teach.

- Through the Patient Protection and Affordable Care Act, also known as Obamacare, the federal government is forcing religious organizations to provide insurance for birth control and abortion-inducing drugs in direct violation of their religious beliefs.

- The US Department of Veterans Affairs banned the mention of God from veterans' funerals, overriding the wishes of the deceased's families.

- A federal judge held that prayers before a state House of Representatives could be to Allah but not to Jesus.[5]

Attacks on Christians are increasing, just as Jesus promised. Hatred of Christ's followers, increasing wickedness, and the rise in false prophets—these are signs that history is coming to a climax. After these trends reach their highest pitch, Jesus said, "the end will come."

TWELVE

God's Peace Treaty

L ESS THAN A WEEK after 9/11, as the wreckage of the World Trade Center still smoldered, President George W. Bush went to the Islamic Center in Washington, DC. He stood with leaders of the American Muslim community and said:

> These acts of violence against innocents violate the fundamental tenets of the Islamic faith. And it's important for my fellow Americans to understand that.
>
> The English translation is not as eloquent as the original Arabic, but let me quote from the Koran, itself: "In the long run, evil in the extreme will be the end of those who do evil. For that they rejected the signs of Allah and held them up to ridicule."
>
> The face of terror is not the true faith of Islam. That's not what Islam is all about. Islam is peace.[1]

In 2007, Bush made a similar statement in an interview with Al Arabiya reporter Elie Nakouzi:

I believe in an Almighty God, and I believe that all the world, whether they be Muslim, Christian, or any other religion, prays to the same God. That's what I believe. I believe that Islam is a great religion that preaches peace. . . . And I believe people who murder the innocent to achieve political objectives aren't religious people. . . .

And I just simply don't subscribe to the idea that murdering innocent men, women and children—particularly Muslim men, women and children in the Middle East—is an act of somebody who is a religious person."[2]

The problem with Mr. Bush's statement is that facts are facts, whether we choose to "subscribe" to them or not.

Our three most recent presidents—Presidents Clinton, Bush, and Obama—have all called Islam "a religion of peace" in an effort to distinguish between Islamic terrorists and "moderate" (i.e., nonviolent) Muslims. But it's important to realize that some of the most powerful and influential leaders in the Islamic world do not make that distinction. For example, Turkish prime minister Recep Tayyip Erdoğan once called the term *moderate Islam* a "very ugly" term. "It is offensive and an insult to our religion," he said. "There is no moderate or immoderate Islam. Islam is Islam and that's it."[3]

One of the most common misconceptions Westerners have about Islam is the notion that *Islam* means "peace." As we've already noted, *Islam* comes from the Arabic root word *aslama,* which means "surrender," not peace. The word *aslama* is related to *salaam* only in that they have a common consonant sound, but Islam (*aslama*) does not derive from *salaam* ("peace") in any way. Though there are a few small pacifist offshoots of Islam (such as the Ahmadiyya sect in India and the Alevi sect in Turkey), mainstream Islamic law is filled with rules and regulations for the use of violence to punish wrongdoing within a family, within the Islamic community, or when waging war.

Pastor and journalist Michael Carl criticizes the notion he calls "Islam Lite"—the idea that there is a "moderate" or "lite" Islam that is a "religion of peace." Many Christians, with the best of intentions, are easily duped by propaganda groups like CAIR (the Council on American-Islamic Relations). Carl explains:

> Christians are of course commanded by Christ to "make disciples of all nations." So it's commendable . . . [that Christians seek a dialogue with] Muslims. But that's not the objective the Muslims have in mind. The CAIR sponsored groups . . . present "Islam Lite" to the unaware Christians in the audience. They speak of faithfulness to Allah, pilgrimages, doing charitable works and Christians just soak it up not knowing that there is a double edge on those Islamic terms and concepts. . . .
>
> A good example of this is Muslim writer Yahiya Emerick. Emerick has written *The Complete Idiot's Guide to Understanding Islam*. This is his work that

presents Islam Lite, the "Islam is a religion of peace" . . . version. This is the book that presents Islam as "just like Christianity because they go to their mosque, have an Islamic version of Sunday School for the kids," etc. Then there's Yahiya Emerick's textbook that he wrote for seventh grade students in Islamic schools. In this book, . . . [Emerick] tells Muslim students that the Bible is a book of fables and myths, that jihad really means conquering infidels and that all Muslims have a duty to support jihad.[4]

Much of the confusion over the goals of Islam lies in the definition of "peace." When the apologists of Islam tell us that Islam is a "religion of peace," they probably mean it with all sincerity—but as Michael Carl points out, the word *peace* often has a "double edge" when it is used by Muslims. *Peace* has one meaning for Christians—but a very different meaning for Islamists.

Delusion and Confusion

Christians know Jesus as "the Prince of Peace" (Isaiah 9:6). When Gideon built an altar to the Lord, he called the altar Jehovah-Shalom, "The LORD is Peace" (Judges 6:24). "In peace I will lie down and sleep," wrote the Psalmist (4:8). "The LORD blesses his people with peace" (Psalm 29:11). And before Jesus went to the cross, He told His followers, "Peace I leave with you; my peace I give you" (John 14:27). God's perfect peace is a major theme throughout the Old and New Testaments.

Islam also speaks of peace. Muslims traditionally greet one another with the words "*Salaam alaikum*," meaning, "Peace to you." Yet if you read through the Koran, you'll notice that it has very little to say about peace. Though the theme of God's peace runs like a mighty river through the Old Testament and the New Testament, there is no corresponding theme of "the peace of Allah" in the Koran.

In one of the few Koranic passages that mentions peace at all, we read: "(Allah has knowledge) of the (Prophet's) cry, 'O my Lord! Truly these are people who will not believe!' But turn away from them, and say 'Peace!' But soon shall they know!" (Koran 43:88–89). In other words, Allah tells Muhammad, in effect, "If you meet unbelievers, just say 'Peace' to them and go your own way, don't get into a religious debate with them—but sooner or later, they'll find out!" In one of the rare instances where the Koran mentions peace, the word has an ominous undertone.

Everywhere we look we see clashes, terrorist attacks, disasters, tragedies, and killings. We see nations at war with each other, East battling West, Islamists attacking Jews and Christians, political parties at war with each other, family members at war with each other. Looking within, we see that we are even at war with ourselves—we are addicted to behaviors we hate, we are angry and frustrated with ourselves, we are powerless to do the good we want to do.

There is no peace in the world around us, and no peace within us. When the angels announced the birth of Jesus, they said, "Glory to God in the highest heaven, and on earth peace to those on whom his favor rests" (Luke 2:14). But where is this peace on earth that the angels promised? Where is the peace that the baby in the stable was supposed to bring? With every Christmas that goes by, that promised peace seems more and more elusive.

Perhaps the core of the problem lies in our definition of *peace*. Perhaps we have a semantic problem, a comprehension problem. Maybe the problem is not with God's promise but with our perception. Maybe we have misunderstood and misdefined what it means to have peace on earth.

I believe there are actually three forms of peace. One is the kind of peace the world knows. One is the kind of peace Islam offers. And one is the kind of peace that Jesus, the Prince of Peace, offers. Those three kinds of peace are deceptive peace, dark peace, and divine peace. Let's look at these three forms of peace and clear away our delusion and confusion.

Deceptive Peace— The "Peace" the World Offers

Deceptive peace is the state of being mentally and emotionally lulled—a state of tranquility, of being serene and quiet and sedate. There are many ways to achieve a deceptive peace. We can take alcohol or drugs to numb our senses and put us in a sedated, passive state. A deceptive peace tranquilizes our senses, deadens our emotions, and blurs our reality.

The deceptive power of mind-altering, mood-altering drugs knows no bounds. One day in November 1960, Harvard psychology professor Timothy Leary gave some psilocybin—a drug derived from psychedelic mushrooms— to a beatnik poet named Allen Ginsberg. Instantly, Ginsberg was seized by hallucinations of deceptive peace.

"We're going down to the city streets and tell the people about peace and love," Ginsberg proclaimed to Leary. He picked up the phone and told the operator he was God, and he tried to telephone his dead mother. Then he told Leary that he had a plan for bringing about world peace by secretly slipping psilocybin to President John F. Kennedy and Soviet premier Nikita Khrushchev. After Ginsberg came down from his drug trip, he and Leary planned out the coming "psychedelic revolution."[5] Together, Leary and Ginsberg set in motion the hippie movement of the 1960s—the "peace, love, and rock and roll" delusion that culminated in Woodstock and the Manson murders.

Getting high doesn't bring us peace. An entire generation got high, but drugs didn't bring an end to the Vietnam War or prevent any of the wars that followed. John Lennon sang, "Give peace a chance."[6] But the peace he sang about is the peace the world brings, and it's a delusional, deceptive peace.

Another form of deceptive peace is political peace—the kind of peace that takes place when two rival nations sign a sheet of paper and declare "peace." In September 1938, the prime minister of Great Britain, Neville Chamberlain, went to Munich, Germany, and met with the German chancellor, Adolf Hitler. They worked out the Munich Agreement, which gave Germany a portion of Czechoslovakia in exchange for a promise of peace. After Hitler signed the agreement, he privately told his foreign minister, "Oh, don't take it all so seriously. That piece of paper is of no significance whatsoever."[7]

Mr. Chamberlain rushed back to England, saying he had achieved "peace with honour," adding, "I believe it is peace for our time."[8]

The following spring, Hitler invaded more Czech provinces. In the fall of 1939, Hitler invaded Poland, trampling the last shreds of the false "peace" he had made with Neville Chamberlain—and World War II began.

Political peace is a deceptive peace. The moment we think we have achieved "peace for our time," it crumbles to dust.

Another form of deceptive peace is when we use escapist media to numb ourselves to reality. There's nothing wrong with a little relaxation and entertainment now and then— but some people waste hour after hour watching movies or TV, immersing themselves in social media on the Internet, or obsessively checking their smartphones. Our entertainment technologies enable us to enter a dreamlike state where we don't have to acknowledge the realities of life, including spiritual reality. It's a substitute peace, a deceptive peace. But a deceptive peace doesn't satisfy and it cannot last. We can hide from reality for a little while, but we can't escape it forever.

The only peace this world offers is a deceptive peace.

Dark Peace—The "Peace" of Islam

I want to make this very clear: From a certain point of view, Islam *is* "a religion of peace." It simply depends on how you define *peace*. Under Islamic Sharia law, you can absolutely have "peace." But be advised: it's a dark peace.

The peace of Islam is the dark peace that comes after the war against non-Muslims is won and all the "infidels" have been conquered and subjugated. It's a peace that comes after the women have been enslaved and the children oppressed. It's the peace that comes after one side surrenders, bows in submission, and agrees to all the terms imposed by the conqueror.

When President George W. Bush gave his post-9/11 "Islam is peace" speech at the Islamic Center in Washington, DC, CAIR cofounder Nihad Awad—a man with ties to Hamas and the Muslim Brotherhood—stood behind him, nodding agreement. And Nihad Awad could undoubtedly endorse much of what Mr. Bush said. Awad would agree that "Islam is peace"—because he defines "peace" differently than Mr. Bush does.

In his book *Religion of Peace?*, Robert Spencer explains:

Warfare against unbelievers . . . is the [Koran's] last word on jihad. Mainstream Islamic tradition has interpreted this as Allah's enduring marching orders to the human race: the Islamic umma (community) must exist in a state of perpetual war, punctuated only by temporary truces, with the non-Muslim world. These are very different from the marching orders Jesus gave His apostles in the "Great Commission" of the New Testament: "Therefore go and make disciples of all nations, baptizing them in the name of the Father and of the Son and of the Holy Spirit;" Muslims, given the final instructions of Allah to Muhammad, were to compel conversion or subjugation through holy war: jihad.[9]

How do we attain the peace that Islam offers us? It's simple. All we have to do is either surrender our souls by becoming Muslims—or surrender our freedom by submissively paying the jizya, the religious tax all non-Muslims must pay to prove that they meekly accept the Islamic rule and Sharia law.

This is why it's important we understand that *Islam* does not mean "peace." It means "surrender." The dark peace of Islam is ours when we give up the fight, deny that Jesus is Lord, and surrender to Islamic oppression.

Divine Peace—The Peace of Jesus Christ

Neither deceptive peace nor dark peace is the kind of peace the angels announced to the shepherds at the first Christmas. God didn't send His beloved Son into the world to bring us a peace that is momentary, temporary, illusory, deceptive, or dark and oppressive. Jesus came into the world to liberate us from death and sin, and to bring us peace with God— the peace that passes understanding, the peace that calms our fears, even in times of trouble. As Jesus told His disciples, "I have told you these things, so that in me you may have peace. In this world you will have trouble. But take heart! I have overcome the world" (John 16:33).

The peace that Jesus brings is divine peace, the peace of God, the only peace worthy of the name. Divine peace is the only permanent peace. Divine peace is that kind of peace you feel inside even when the world is falling apart all around you. Divine peace is peace of mind, peace in your conscience, peace with your Christian brothers and sisters, peace with your boss and coworkers, peace with your environment, peace with your world.

This is the peace the angels announced. It's the peace Jesus exemplified. When you have divine peace, you can have peace while the wars are raging around you, peace while the earth is crumbling beneath your feet, peace in the midst of the storm.

In Mark 4, Jesus crossed over the Sea of Galilee in a boat with His disciples. He was in the back of the boat, sleeping on a pillow, when a storm arose and the waves lashed the boat. Soon the boat was filling with water—yet Jesus remained peacefully asleep. The disciples woke Him and said, "Teacher, don't you care if we drown?" (Mark 4:38).

Then Jesus got up and spoke to the waves: "Peace, be still" (Mark 4:39 KJV). And the winds ceased and the waters became calm.

That is divine peace in action. That is the peace Jesus offers to you and me amid the storms of this life. When the whole world is panicking, we have peace. When the whole world turns against us, we have peace. When the signs of the end times begin to appear, when there are wars and rumors of wars, when nations rise against each other, when there are famines and earthquakes, we are not alarmed. We have divine peace.

When we are handed over to be persecuted and hated and killed because of Jesus, we have divine peace. When people turn away from the faith and betray us, when false teachers appear and deceive many people, when the love of most people grows cold, we have divine peace. And even when we see the abomination that causes desolation standing in the holy place, as the prophet Daniel predicted, even when it is time to flee to the mountains, even when there is great distress, unequaled from the beginning of time until now, we have divine peace.

Jesus said in Matthew 24:23–24, "If anyone says to you, 'Look, here is the Messiah!' or, 'There he is!' do not believe it. For false messiahs and false prophets will appear and perform great signs and wonders to deceive, if possible, even the elect." But you and I need not be deceived by false messiahs and false prophets, because we have divine peace—and we refuse to be stampeded and fooled by the deceivers who will arise in the Last Days.

When you have peace with God, you have the peace of Christ that transcends human understanding. Even if the sun and moon turn dark and the stars are shaken from the sky, we can sleep peacefully, knowing that Jesus, who commands the winds and the waves with His word, is the Lord of the earth and sky. He slept soundly in the middle of the storm—and so can we.

Jesus never promised us a life without problems. He told us to expect trouble and persecution. He told us that the Last Days would be full of turbulence and testing. He told us that the world would hate us, put us on trial, and put us to death. But we have divine peace.

When you have divine peace, you are like a submarine in a hurricane. If you remain on the surface, you'll be destroyed—but if you dive deep into the ocean of God's love, you'll have peace. No, you won't escape your circumstances completely. Even if a submarine descends to a depth of four hundred feet, it can feel the rocking motion of the waves above. A hurricane-force storm on the surface can cause a submarine to roll ten to fifteen degrees—enough to make some sub-mariners seasick. But the crew will be safe beneath the waves, because it has gone deep, deep, deep, where the turbulent storm cannot destroy it.

That is what divine peace is like. It doesn't mean the storm won't rock your boat. It doesn't guarantee you won't get seasick. But it does guarantee peace that passes understand-ing, peace that transcends comprehension, peace that defies explanation. It's the peace that only the Lord Jesus Christ can bring you. It's a peace that can't be found in the secular world or in Islam. It can be found in Jesus alone.

Many cry out for peace. Many struggle with guilt and fear. Their consciences are a war zone. Their minds are a battlefield. Their relationships are stormy seas. Their hearts are filled with anxiety and confusion. That's why Jesus said, "Peace I leave with you; my peace I give you. I do not give to you as the world gives. Do not let your hearts be troubled and do not be afraid" (John 14:27).

All the money in the world can't buy you a moment of divine peace. All the good works and charitable deeds and religious rituals in the world will never buy you God's peace. You can't earn it or inherit it or ever be worthy of it—but you can have it for free. Divine peace is a gift.

Islam and "The Peace Child"

In 1976, I was serving in a church in Australia. A friend called and asked if I would host a Canadian missionary who had been serving in the remote regions of Irian Jaya (West Papua Province), the western part of the island of New Guinea. That missionary's name was Don Richardson, and it was a delight to get to know him.

In those days, I had no idea of the amazing missionary journey of Don and Carol Richardson. In 1962, they went to New Guinea to work among the Sawi people, a tribe of cannibalistic headhunters. The Richardsons trusted God to protect them not only from the Sawi themselves, but from the malaria and other diseases that were rampant in the rain forest.

The Sawi language was difficult to master. Don soon learned that there are nineteen tenses for every Sawi verb. But cultural differences turned out to be an even bigger barrier than the language differences. When Don tried to explain the gospel story to the Sawi, he learned that they regarded treachery and deception as a virtue. When he told them the story of Judas betraying Jesus for thirty pieces of silver, they applauded Judas as the hero. His attempt to present Jesus as Lord and Redeemer met with laughter and derision.

The warlike nature of the Sawi was another problem. Don and Carol had tried to get the tribespeople of three Sawi villages to come together in one peaceful community—but their efforts backfired, and it seemed that full-scale tribal war might break out any day. The Richardsons decided they needed to leave—not out of concern for their own safety, but to enable the three villages to return to their state of isolation from one another and reduce the risk of violence.

When the Sawi heard that the Richardsons planned to leave, they begged the couple not to go. The Sawi even promised that they would make peace between the villages if the Richardsons would stay. So Don and Carol Richardson arose at dawn to watch the Sawi peace ritual—and what they witnessed was astonishing and deeply moving.

In each village, a family was chosen—and that family had to send a child to live with a family in the other village. As long as the child lived, peace would continue. But it was hard to find a family willing to make that heart-wrenching sacrifice.

Finally, one tearful father picked up his son—his *only* child—and rushed to hand the boy over to his enemies. The enemy villagers selected a child and gave that child in trade—and so the Sawi villages established peace.

Watching this scene, Don Richardson was struck by a realization. He had just seen a beautiful reenactment of the Christian gospel. The village child was called "the peace child." The Sawi expected deception and treachery from one another—but if a man would give his own son to his enemies, he proved he could be trusted. No tribesman would ever attack a neighboring village if his own son lived in that village.

Don Richardson began teaching the Sawi people about a Father who gave His only Son to the human race while they were His enemies. God proved He could be trusted by sending His only Son to live among us. Jesus is the Peace Child, the Prince of Peace, who brings peace with God.

The Richardsons stayed in the village, and they saw many Sawi people give their lives to Jesus Christ as Lord and Savior. Carol used her nursing skills to treat patients and teach hygiene while Don evangelized, translated the New Testament, and taught the people how to read.

In a 2003 interview with *Christianity Today*, Don Richardson talked about how, in recent years, he had studied the Koran and the Islamic religion, searching for some analogy (similar to the "peace child" analogy) that Christians might use to reach Muslims with the gospel. Unfortunately, he couldn't find even one. Why not? Because Muhammad, in the Koran, had redefined every core Christian truth, thus inoculating his followers against the gospel. Don explained:

If you're going to lead someone to understand Jesus as the Messiah, the one who by his reconciling death provided an atonement for mankind, [you have a problem because] the [Koran] says Jesus didn't die. He was just a prophet. There was no atonement.

> [If] you're going to talk about heaven . . . Muhammad redefined heaven as what you might call an enormous bordello in the sky.
>
> Heaven is redefined. The work of Jesus on earth is redefined. Even the very nature of God is recast by Muhammad.[10]

Islam seems to have been deliberately designed to plunge millions of people into spiritual darkness—and to keep them there by preventing them from ever even considering the truth about Jesus Christ. As we have seen, Islam seems intentionally crafted to prepare Muslims to receive the Antichrist as their long-prophesied Mahdi. The Koran's teachings seem carefully calculated to blind people to the good news of Jesus Christ and to prepare the way for the powerful delusion of the Last Days.

The struggle we face is not primarily a war on terror or a battle against Islamic extremists or jihadism. Our struggle is a spiritual struggle—not a war against flesh and blood, but against the rulers, powers, and spiritual forces of this dark world (Ephesians 6:12).

Surrender Your Weapon

In 1970, I worked for the telephone company in Sydney, Australia. I had only been in the country for a few months, and I had arrived with only one hundred dollars of borrowed money in my pocket. My boss at the phone company knew my impoverished state. One day, he came to me and said, "Michael, may I ask you a personal question? Tell me—why do you seem so peaceful and contented? You have almost nothing. You're just scraping by. Yet you never complain, you never seem worried, you seem to be at peace."

"I am at peace," I said. "I know that God is in charge of all the circumstances of my life. When I received Jesus as Lord of my life, I surrendered everything to Him—my plans and goals, my finances, my circumstances, even my worries and anxiety. I surrendered it all to Him, and in exchange for that, He has given me peace."

My boss thought for a moment, then he said something that saddens me to this day: "I couldn't do that, Michael. I could never surrender my will to anyone."

I had a number of talks with this man while I worked at the phone company. I found out that he knew the Christian gospel, and he occasionally went to church—but he had never surrendered his life to the Lord. He was unwilling to put God in charge of his life.

He saw with his own eyes that surrendering to Christ had brought peace to my life—a peace that passes understanding, a peace that he himself could not understand. Though he wanted that peace, he refused to pay the price of surrendering himself to God.

Isn't it ironic? Islam, which is falsely called "the religion of peace," is actually a religion called "surrender." And once you surrender to Islam, the only "peace" you'll know is a dark and oppressive peace, the peace of defeat and subjugation.

But if we surrender to Jesus, the Prince of Peace, we receive a *real* peace, God's peace, the peace that passes understanding.

Only Jesus can give you that peace, and it's a paradoxical peace because it's free—you can't earn it or deserve it or buy it. But to obtain this free gift, you have to surrender. You have to give up and let Jesus take over control of your life. You have to surrender your weapons.

You may say, "But I don't have any weapons."

Every one of us has a weapon, and the weapon you must surrender is your *will*. Your selfish wants, your ambitions, your determination to do everything your way—surrender your weapon. Your insistence on living to gratify your appetite for pleasure, material things, money, fame, and the applause of others—surrender your weapon. The drinking or drugs or gambling or pornography or adultery or other guilty pleasure you cling to—surrender your weapon. Your spitefulness, your bitterness, your blaming, your vengefulness, your anger, your lashing out at others—surrender your weapon.

Gratefully accept the free gift of salvation and lay down your weapons. You will be accepted and welcomed into God's family, now and forever.

You might be thinking, *When things get really bad, when world events seem so hopeless that the Lord's return seems imminent, then I'll make my peace with God.* My friend, life is uncertain, and you may never get another chance to come to Him. Why don't you come to Him now? He is waiting for you.

When the Lord returns, His timing will be sudden and unexpected. Only those who are watching and waiting for Him will rejoice. The rest will despair and ask, "Why did I wait? Why didn't I say yes to Jesus when I had the chance?" In the Olivet Discourse, Jesus described how swift and sudden His return would be:

> As it was in the days of Noah, so it will be at the coming of the Son of Man. For in the days before the flood, people were eating and drinking, marrying and giving in marriage, up to the day Noah entered the ark; and they knew nothing about what would happen until the flood came and took them all away. That is how it will be at the coming of the Son of Man. Two men will be in the field; one will be taken and the other left. Two women will be grinding with a hand mill; one will be taken and the other left.
>
> Therefore keep watch, because you do not know on what day your Lord will come. (Matthew 24:37–42)

When the Lord returns, those who are taken will live forever in heaven with Jesus. Those who are left behind must await the judgment. When is Jesus returning? Nobody knows the hour—but He could return before you finish reading this page.

Don't put off the decision. Decide now—then keep watch for His return. Live each day with a sense of urgency and expectancy.

Jesus prophesied the destruction of the temple in Jerusalem. It was an unbelievable prediction. No one believed that this magnificent building could be destroyed, so that not one stone was left upon another. But the Lord's prophecy was fulfilled with absolute accuracy in AD 70 during the Roman siege of Jerusalem.

Other signs that Jesus predicted still remain to be fulfilled. But make no mistake about it—those prophecies will be fulfilled with equal precision and accuracy. The Lord will keep every one of His promises, including His promise of our salvation and redemption. As Paul writes, "Therefore, since we have these promises, dear friends, let us purify ourselves from everything that contaminates body and spirit, perfecting holiness out of reverence for God" (2 Corinthians 7:1).

My heart aches for the Muslim who works hard, maintaining all the rituals, trying to earn Allah's mercy. He has no promise of salvation, no assurance of peace. He faithfully keeps the Five Pillars of Islam, he recites the Shahadah, he prays five times a day, he pays the zakat to the poor, he fasts during Ramadan, he makes his pilgrimage to Mecca—and after he has done all that, he still has no assurance that Allah will be merciful. He never knows if he has done enough to earn Allah's favor. Islam is surrender without any guarantee of peace.

In contrast, the gospel of Jesus Christ is the story of a God who loves us, who knew we could do nothing to save ourselves, who knew that we were lost in our sin, mired in our strife—so He gave us His peace. In His infinite mercy, God sent His Son to earth. Jesus left the glories of heaven and came to us to atone for our sin, to pay our debt, to meet our obligations, to exchange our strife for His peace. Jesus made the sacrifice. All you and I have to do is say, "I surrender, Lord, to Your love."

223

Then—and only then—will you receive the gift of divine peace. Only when you come to Him in gratitude and thanksgiving, accepting His sacrifice on the cross for you, will you know the peace that passes all human comprehension and understanding. Church membership won't bring you divine peace. Intellectually assenting to Christian doctrines won't bring you divine peace. Even admiring Jesus as a great prophet and teacher won't bring you divine peace.

When you surrender your life to Jesus, He gives you His divine peace. Jesus surrendered His glory in heaven so that you might live forever with Him. He has done all that to bring you His peace. All He asks is that you surrender to His love.

What will your answer be?

Notes

Introduction: A Wake-Up Call

1. Nour Malas and Maria Abi-Habib, "Islamic State Economy Runs on Extortion, Oil Piracy in Syria, Iraq," *Wall Street Journal*, August 28, 2014, http://online.wsj.com/articles/islamic-state-fills-coffers-from-illicit -economy-in-syria-iraq-1409175458.

2. Stoyan Zaimov, "ISIS' Beheadings, Crucifixion, Stonings Witnessed by 13-Year-Old; Terror Group Indoctrinating Young Minds," *Christian Post*, September 1, 2014, http://www.christianpost.com /news/isis-beheadings-crucifixion-stonings-witnessed-by-13-year -old-terror-group-indoctrinating-young-minds-125656/; Bob Unruh, "Faith Under Fire: 5-Year-Old Christian Boy Cut in Half by ISIS," World Net Daily, August 12, 2014, http://mobile.wnd.com/2014/08 /5-year-old-christian-boy-cut-in-half-by-isis/.

Chapter 1: The Goal of World Domination

1. Kareem Fahim, "Slap to a Man's Pride Set Off Tumult in Tunisia," *New York Times*, January 21, 2011, http://www.nytimes.com/2011/01/22/world /africa/22sidi.html?_r=2&src=twrhp&pagewanted=all; Peter Beaumont, "Mohammed Bouazizi: The Dutiful Son Whose Death Changed Tunisia's Fate," *The Guardian*, January 20, 2011, http://www.guardian .co.uk/world/2011/jan/20/tunisian-fruit-seller-mohammed-bouazizi.

2. Yasmine Ryan, "The Tragic Life of a Street Vendor," Al Jazeera English, January 20, 2011, http://english.aljazeera.net/indepth /features/2011/01/201111684242518839.html.

3. Bob Simon, "How a Slap Sparked Tunisia's Revolution," CBS News, February 22, 2011, produced by Draggan Mihailovich and Nathalie

Sommer, *60 Minutes*, http://www.cbsnews.com/stories/2011/02/20/60minutes/main20033404.shtml.

4. BBC, "Tunisia Suicide Protester Mohammed Bouazizi Dies," BBC News, January 5, 2011, http://www.bbc.co.uk/news/world-africa-12120228.

5. Can Ertuna, "The Regime is Overthrown, What Now?," *Hurriyet Daily News*, February 15, 2011, http://www.hurriyetdailynews.com/default.aspx?pageid=438&n=the-regime-is-overthrown-what-now-2011-02-15.

6. Amro Hassan, "Egypt: Some Copts and Muslims Come Together during Orthodox Christmas," *Babylon and Beyond* (blog), *Los Angeles Times*, January 8, 2011, http://latimesblogs.latimes.com/babylonbeyond/2011/01/egypt-copts-and-muslims-come-together-for-once-during-orthodox-christmas.html.

7. Nevine Zaki, "Christians Protect Muslims during Prayer in Cairo's Dangerous Tahrir Square," PhotoBlog on MSNBC.com, February 3, 2011, http://photoblog.msnbc.msn.com/_news/2011/02/03/5981906-christians-protect-muslims-during-prayer-in-cairos-dangerous-tahrir-square. Photo also available at *Daily Mail Reporter*, "Images of solidarity as Christians join hands to protect Muslims as they pray during Cairo protests," February 3, 2011, http://www.dailymail.co.uk/news/article-1353330/Egypt-protests-Christians-join-hands-protect-Muslims-pray-Cairo-protests.html.

8. "Egypt Clashes: Copts Mourn Victims of Cairo Unrest," BBC News, October 10, 2011, http://www.bbc.co.uk/news/world-middle-east-15242413.

9. Associated Press, "Coptic Christian Priest Killed in Southern Egypt," ABC News, February 23, 2011, http://news.yahoo.com/coptic-christian-priest-killed-southern-egypt-20110223-014732-949.html.

10. Reza Sayah, "Egypt's Military Begins Rebuilding Burned Coptic Church," CNN, March 13, 2011, http://www.cnn.com/2011/WORLD/meast/03/13/egypt.church/index.html.

11. "Egypt Clashes: Copts Mourn," http://www.bbc.co.uk/news/world-middle-east-15242413.

12. AFP, "Egypt Copts Protest over Church Burning, Blogger," Africa Review, October 5, 2011, http://www.africareview.com/News/Egypt-Copts-protest-over-church-burning-blogger/-/979180/1248276/-/wvgptn/-/index.html.

13. Mary Abdelmassih, "Muslims Attack Christian in Egypt, Cut Off His Ear," Assyrian International News Agency, March 26, 2011, http://www.aina.org/news/20110325223845.htm.

14. David D. Kirkpatrick, "Church Protests in Cairo Turn Deadly," *New York Times*, October 9, 2011, http://www.nytimes.com/2011/10/10/world /middleeast/deadly-protests-over-church-attack-in-cairo.html ?pagewanted=all.

15. Nawar Shora, *The Arab-American Handbook: A Guide to the Arab, Arab-American, and Muslim Worlds* (Seattle: Cune Press, 2009), 291.

16. Robin Hallett, *Africa Since 1875: A Modern History* (Ann Arbor: University of Michigan Press, 1974), 139.

17. Ian Johnson, *A Mosque in Munich: Nazis, the CIA, and the Rise of the Muslim Brotherhood in the West* (New York: Houghton Mifflin, 2010), 112–13.

18. Mehran Kamrava, *The Modern Middle East: A Political History since the First World War*, 2nd ed. (Berkeley: University of California Press, 2011), 94–95.

19. Lawrence Wright, "The Counter-Terrorist," *New Yorker*, January 14, 2002, http://www.newyorker.com/archive/2002/01/14/020114fa _fact_wright?currentPage=1.

20. Dan Collins, "FBI Was Warned About Flight Schools," CBS News, May 15, 2002, http://www.cbsnews.com/stories/2002/05/15/attack /main509113.shtml; Brian Ross and Lisa Sylvester, "Bush Warned of Hijackings Before 9-11," ABC News, May 15, 2002, http://abcnews .go.com/US/story?id=91651&page=1; National Commission on Terrorist Attacks Upon the United States, "The Attack Looms," chap. 7 in *The 9/11 Commission Report*, August 21, 2004, http://www.9-11commission.gov /report/911Report_Ch7.htm.

21. Lorenzo Vidino, *The New Muslim Brotherhood in the West* (New York: Columbia University Press, 2010), 91.

22. Josh Gerstein, "DNI Clapper Retreats From 'Secular' Claim on Muslim Brotherhood," *Under the Radar* (blog), *Politico*, February 10, 2011, http://www.politico.com/blogs/joshgerstein/0211/DNI_Clapper _Egypts_Muslim_Brotherhood_largely_secular.html.

23. Raven Clabough, "Self-avowed Muslim Marxist Says White House Tied to Muslim Brotherhood," *New American*, August 18, 2011, http://www.thenewamerican.com/usnews/politics/item/9582-self

-avowed-muslim-marxist-says-white-house-tied-to-muslim
-brotherhood.

24. Ibid.

25. Josh Gerstein, "Obama Prayer Speaker Has Hamas Tie?" *Politico*, January 17, 2009, http://www.politico.com/news/stories/0109/17562.html.

26. "Underpublicized Threat Deep in White House," *World Net Daily*, August 27, 2011, http://www.wnd.com/?pageId=337321. See also Michael Youssef, *Blindsided: The Radical Islamic Conquest* (Atlanta: Kobri, 2012), 29.

27. Walid Phares, "US Aid to the Arab Spring Must Go to Democracy Groups Not to Islamists," Accuracy in Media, May 26, 2011, http://www.aim.org/guest-column/u-s-aid-to-arab-spring-must-go-to -democracy-groups-not-to-islamists/.

28. Lucy Ballinger and Dan Newling, "Guilty? It's a Badge of Honour Say Muslim Hate Mob," *Mail* Online, January 12, 2010, http://www .dailymail.co.uk/news/article-1242335/Muslims-called-British -soldiers-rapists-cowards-scum-exercising-freedom-speech-court -hears.html.

29. Watson Institute, "Economic Costs Summary: $3.1 Trillion and Counting," CostsOfWar.org, June 2014, http://costsofwar.org/article /economic-cost-summary; Watson Institute, "U.S. and Allied Killed and Wounded," CostsOfWar.org, June 2014, http://costsofwar.org/article /us-and-allied-killed-and-wounded.

Chapter 2: Ignored Warnings

1. Sayyid Qutb, "'The America I Have Seen': In the Scale of Human Values," (PDF document, Sociology of Islam and Muslim Societies (Portland: Portland Portland State University, 1951), http://www.pdx.edu /sites/www.pdx.edu.sociologyofislam/files/The%20America%20I%20 Have%20Seen%20Sayyid%20Qutb%20Ustad.pdf.

2. Malise Ruthven, *A Fury for God: The Islamist Attack on America* (London: Granta Books, 2004), 75.

3. Sayyid Qutb, "'The America I Have Seen': In the Scale of Human Values."

4. Tony Blankely, *The West's Last Chance: Will We Win the Clash of Civilizations?* (Washington, DC: Regnery, 2005), 181.

5. Robert Spencer, "Sayyid Qutb and the Virginia Five," Frontpage Mag, December 18, 2009, http://www.frontpagemag.com/2009 /robert-spencer/sayyid-qutb-and-the-virginia-five-by-robert-spencer/.

6. Robert Siegel, "Sayyid Qutb's America: Al-Qaeda Inspiration Denounced U.S. Greed, Sexuality," All Things Considered, NPR.org, May 6, 2003, http://www.npr.org/templates/story/story.php?storyId=1253796; "Is This the Man Who Inspired Bin Laden? Robert Irwin on Sayyid Qutb, the Father of Modern Islamist Fundamentalism," *Guardian*, October 31, 2001, http://www.guardian.co.uk/world/2001/nov/01/afghanistan .terrorism3.

7. Lawrence Wright, *The Looming Tower: Al-Qaeda and the Road to 9/11* (New York: Vintage, 2007), 33–34.

8. Ibid., 35.

9. Ibid., 36.

10. Ibid., 34.

11. Ibid., 248.

12. Ibid., 140.

13. Ibid., 150–52.

14. Ibid., 165.

15. Douglas Jehl, "A Nation Challenged: Saudi Arabia; Holy War Lured Saudis As Rulers Looked Away," New York Times, December 27, 2001, http://www.nytimes.com/2001/12/27/world/a-nation-challenged-saudi -arabia-holy-war-lured-saudis-as-rulers-looked-away.html?pagewanted=all.

16. Michael Scheuer, *Through Our Enemies' Eyes: Osama bin Laden, Radical Islam, and the Future of America* (Washington, DC: Potomac Books, 2006), 158.

17. Newsdesk, "Bin Laden's Fatwa," PBS NewsHour, PBS.org, August 23, 1996, http://www.pbs.org/newshour/updates/military -july-dec96-fatwa_1996/.

18. PBS, "Bin Laden v. the U.S.: Edicts and Statements," PBS Frontline, PBS.org, April 1999, http://www.pbs.org/wgbh/pages/frontline/shows /binladen/who/edicts.html.

19. Rudy Giuliani, "Rudy Giuliani on Homeland Security," *Meet the Press*, On The Issues.org, December 9, 2007, http://www.ontheissues.org /Archive/2008_Meet_the_Press_Rudy_Giuliani.htm.

20. "Interview: Osama Bin Laden," PBS *Frontline*, PBS.org, May 1998, http://www.pbs.org/wgbh/pages/frontline/shows/binladen/who/interview.html.

21. Ibid.

22. Ibid.

23. Queen Rania Al-Abdullah, "Transcript: Queen Rania on Oprah Winfrey Show," Embassy of the Hashemite Kingdom of Jordan, October 5, 2001, http://www.jordanembassyus.org/speech_hmqr10052001.htm. See also Michael Ireland, "Queen Rania Of Jordan Explains 'True Islam' On 'Oprah Winfrey Show,'" Assist News Service, October 11, 2001, http://www.assistnews.net/strategic/s0110036.htm.

24. Jacob Poushter, "Support for al Qaeda was Low Before (and After) Osama bin Laden's Death," Pew Research Center, May 2, 2014, http://www.pewresearch.org/fact-tank/2014/05/02/support-for-al-Qaeda-was-low-before-and-after-osama-bin-ladens-death/.

25. Marc Fisher, "Muslim Students Weigh Questions Of Allegiance," *Washington Post*, October 16, 2001.

26. Ibid.

27. "Africans Split on US Strikes," BBC News, October 9, 2001, http://news.bbc.co.uk/2/hi/1586988.stm.

28. Chris Fontaine, "Protests Against U.S.-Led Attacks Continue Worldwide," *San Bernardino Sun*, October 10, 2001, http://lang.sbsun.com/socal/terrorist/1001/10/terror09.asp.

29. Robin Wright, *Sacred Rage: The Wrath of Militant Islam* (New York: Simon and Schuster, 2001), 21.

Chapter 3: The Prophet and the Koran

1. Sir William Muir and T. H. Weir, *The Life of Mohammed* (Edinburgh: John Grant, 1923), 22.

2. Ibid., 51.

3. Brendan January, *The Iranian Revolution* (Minneapolis: Twenty-First Century Books, 2008), 101.

4. William Montgomery Watt, *Muslim-Christian Encounters: Perceptions and Misperceptions,* Routledge Revivals (New York: Routledge, 2013), 38–39.

5. Reza F. Safa, *Inside Islam: Exposing and Reaching the World of Islam* (Lake Mary, FL: Frontline, 1996), 70.

6. Robert Spencer, *Onward Muslim Soldiers: How Jihad Still Threatens America and the West* (Washington, DC: Regnery, 2003), 5.

7. Isaac ben Abraham, *Islam, Terrorism, and Your Future* (Cleveland, OH: Cedar Hills Press, 2002), 23.

8. Sebastian Maisel and John A. Shoup, eds. *Saudi Arabia and the Gulf Arab States Today: An Encyclopedia of Life in the Arab States*, vol. 1 (Westport, CT: Greenwood, 2009), 301.

Chapter 4: Are Allah and Jehovah the Same God?

1. Bertrand Russell, *Autobiography*. Routledge Classics (New York: Routledge, 2009), 242–43.

2. E. M. Wherry, *A Comprehensive Commentary on the Quran* (Osnabrück, Germany: Otto Zeller Verlag, 1973), 36.

Chapter 5: What Does Islam Teach About the End Times?

1. L. Bevan Jones, *The People of the Mosque: The Study of Islam* (Calcutta: Associated Press, YMCA, 1932), 107.

2. Ibid., 213.

3. Chris Mitchell, *Dateline Jerusalem: An Eyewitness Account of Prophecies Unfolding in the Middle East* (Nashville: Thomas Nelson, 2013), 69–70.

4. Gary Barbknecht, *We the People: An Action Guide* (Indianapolis, Dog Ear Publishing, 2010), 108.

5. Muhammad ibn Izzat and Muhammad Arif, *Al Mahdi and the End of Time* (London: Dar al-Taqwa, 1997), 40.

6. Steven Waldman, "Obama's Fascinating Interview with Cathleen Falsani," Beliefnet.com, November 2008, http://www.beliefnet.com/columnists/stevenwaldman/2008/11/obamas-interview-with-cathleen.html.

7. Jennifer Riley, "Many Born-Again Christians Hold Universalist Views, Barna Finds," *Christian Post*, April 18, 2011, http://www.christianpost.com/news/many-born-again-christians-hold-universalist-view-barna-finds-49883/.

8. Richard Abanes, *Religions of the Stars: What Hollywood Believes and How It Affects You* (Bloomington, MN: Bethany House Publishers, 2009), 35.

Chapter 6: Two Different Prescriptions for Life

1. Jon Swaine, "Steve Jobs 'Regretted Trying to Beat Cancer with Alternative Medicine for so Long,'" *Telegraph*, October 21, 2011, http://www.telegraph.co.uk/technology/apple/8841347/Steve-Jobs-regretted-trying-to-beat-cancer-with-alternative-medicine-for-so-long.html.

2. A. S. Tritton, *The Caliphs and Their Non-Muslim Subjects* (London: Frank Cass and Company, 1970), 5–8.

3. "The World Factbook: Egypt," Central Intelligence Agency, subsection "People and Society," last updated June 22, 2014 https://www.cia.gov /library/publications/the-world-factbook/geos/eg.html.

4. "Bin Laden's Fatwa," *PBS NewsHour*, PBS.org, August 23, 1996, http://www.pbs.org/newshour/updates/military-july-dec96-fatwa_1996/.

Chapter 7: What Is Jihad?

1. Sharona Schwartz, "'My Jihad': CAIR Ad Campaign Tries to Rebrand 'Jihad' as a Positive Word," *The Blaze*, January 7, 2013, http://www .theblaze.com/stories/2013/01/07/my-jihad-cair-ad-campaign-tries-to -rebrand-jihad-as-a-positive-word/.

2. IPT News, "Federal Judge Agrees: CAIR Tied to Hamas," The Investigative Project on Terrorism, November 22, 2010, http://www .investigativeproject.org/2340/federal-judge-agrees-cair-tied-to-hamas.

3. Bruce Bawer, *Surrender: Appeasing Islam, Sacrificing Freedom* (New York: Doubleday, 2009), 81.

4. "WGN 9: Nationwide 'My Jihad' Ad Campaign Launches in Chicago," CAIRChicago.org, December 18, 2012, http://www .cairchicago.org/2012/12/18/wgn-9-nationwide-my-jihad-ad -campaign-launches-in-chicago/.

5. Drew Zahn, "Ad War Erupts Over Meaning of 'Jihad' in U.S.," WND.com, December 16, 2012, http://www.wnd.com/2012/12/ad-war -erupts-over-meaning-of-jihad-in-u-s/.

6. Brad Hughes, "The Worldview War," *American Thinker*, July 16, 2011, http://www.americanthinker.com/2011/07/the_worldview_war.html.

7. Hasan al-Banna, "To What Do We Summon Mankind?" *Five Tracts of Hasan al-Banna*, trans. Charles Wendell (Berkeley: University of California Press, 1978), 80.

8. Gary Bauer, "What is Radical Christianity?" *Human Events*, August 31, 2007, http://www.humanevents.com/2007/08/31/what-is -radical-christianity/.

9. Harvey Cox, "Why Fundamentalism Will Fail," *Boston Globe*, November 8, 2009, http://www.boston.com/bostonglobe/ideas/articles/2009/11/08 /why_fundamentalism_will_fail/?page=full.

10. David Bukay, "The Religious Foundations of Suicide Bombings," *Middle East Quarterly*, Fall 2006, Vol. XIII, No. 4, http://www.meforum.org/1003/the-religious-foundations-of-suicide-bombings#_ftn14.

11. Norman L. Geisler and Abdul Saleeb, *Answering Islam: The Crescent in Light of the Cross* (Grand Rapids: Baker, 2002), 319.

12. Robin Wright, *Sacred Rage: The Wrath of Militant Islam* (New York: Simon and Schuster, 1985), 99.

13. Ibid., 83–84.

14. Hasan al-Banna, "Between Yesterday and Today," *Five Tracts of Hasan al-Banna,* trans. Charles Wendell (Berkeley: University of California Press, 1978), 36.

15. Ishak Ibraham, *Black Gold and Holy War: The Religious Secret Behind the Petrodollar* (Nashville: Thomas Nelson, 1983), 96.

16. Ibid., 31.

17. Ibid., 271.

18. Cathy Reisenwitz, "Who's Afraid of Ayaan Hirsi Ali? Cultural Imperialism and Islamophobia," *Huffington Post*, The Blog, April 14, 2014, http://www.huffingtonpost.com/cathy-reisenwitz/whos-afraid-of-ayaan-hirs_b_5148397.html.

19. Mohamed Akram, "An Explanatory Memorandum on the General Strategic Goal for the Brotherhood in North America," Investigative Project on Terrorism, May 19, 1991, http://www.investigativeproject.org/document/id/20.

20. Danette Clark, "Blog: Boy Scouts of America Infiltrated by Muslim Brotherhood," Klein Online, September 24, 2011, http://kleinonline.wnd.com/2011/09/24/blog-boy-scouts-of-america-infiltrated-by-muslim-brotherhood-trustworthy-loyal-and-helpful-or-destruction-of-western-way-of-life/.

21. "Dr. Muzammil Siddiqi Honored with Human Relations Award," *Muslim Observer*, May 12, 2011, http://muslimmedianetwork.com/mmn/?p=8428.

22. IPT, "Apologists or Extremists: Muzammil Siddiqi," Investigative Project on Terrorism, April 20, 2011, http://www.investigativeproject.org/profile/171.

23. "No to Shariah Compliance Petition—Please Sign," Shariah Finance Watch, June 19, 2008, http://www.shariahfinancewatch.org/blog/2008/06/19/no-to-shariah-compliance-petition-please-sign/.

24. Aaron Klein, "Muslims Sued for Destroying Jewish Temple Artifacts," WND.com, November 9, 2007, http://www.wnd.com/2007/11/44446/.

25. "A Record of Bias: National Public Radio's Coverage of the Arab-Israeli Conflict, September 26–November 26, 2000," CAMERA executive summary, Committee for Acuracy in Middle East Reporting in America, Executive Summary, March 27, 2001, http://www.camera.org/index .asp?x_context=20&x_article=75.

26. Karin McQuillan, "NPR on a Bad Day," *American Thinker*, April 3, 2011, http://www.americanthinker.com/2011/04/npr_on_a_bad_day.html.

Chapter 8: The Global Caliphate

1. Rick Bragg, "A Nation Challenged; Prayers Sustain Pakistani Church in Hard Times," *New York Times*, November 4, 2001, http://www.nytimes .com/2001/11/04/world/a-nation-challenged-prayers-sustain-pakistani -church-in-hard-times.html.

2. Diane Alden, "Christianity Under Siege, Part II: Those Who Are Voiceless," Newsmax.com, January 10, 2002, http://archive.news -max.com/commentmax/get.pl?a=2002/1/9/224114. Also available at http://www.freerepublic.com/focus/fr/610328/posts.

3. Lawrence Haas, "Time to Air Muslim Violence Against Christians," Real Clear Politics, March 23, 2013, http://www.realclearpolitics.com /articles/2012/03/23/time_to_air_muslim_violence_against _christians_113595.html.

4. Ibid.

5. Mary Abdelmassih, "100,000 Christians Have Left Egypt Since March: Report," Assyrian International News Agency, September 26, 2011, http://www.aina.org/news/20110926194822.htm.

6. James Cook, "Sunnis? Shiites? What's That Got to Do With Oil Prices?," *Forbes*, April 12, 1982, 99.

7. Neil MacFarquhar, "A Nation Challenged: Teachings; Bin Laden and His Followers Adhere to an Austere, Stringent Form of Islam," *New York Times*, October 7, 2001, http://www.nytimes.com/2001/10/07/world /nation-challenged-teachings-bin-laden-his-followers-adhere-austere -stringent.html?pagewanted=all.

Chapter 9: All Roads Lead to Israel

1. Brad Plumer, "The U.S. gives Egypt $1.5 Billion a Year in Aid. Here's What It Does," *Washington Post*, Wonkblog, July 9, 2013,

http://www.washingtonpost.com/blogs/wonkblog/wp/2013/07/09
/the-u-s-gives-egypt-1-5-billion-a-year-in-aid-heres-what-it-does/.

2. Yitzhak Benhorin, "Israel Still Top Recipient of US Foreign Aid,"
   Ynet News, February 8, 2007, http://www.ynetnews.com/articles
   /0,7340,L-3362402,00.html.

3. Daniel Wagner and Giorgio Cafiero, "Egypt, Israel and al-Qaeda,"
   Huffington Post, *The Blog*, February 24, 2014, http://www
   .huffingtonpost.com/daniel-wagner/egypt-israel-and-alqaeda_b
   _4846018.html.

4. Dennis Prager, "The Middle East Problem," Prager University video,
   5:40, http://www.prageruniversity.com/Political-Science/Middle-East
   -Problem.html#.U3R6Fyjy33Q.

5. Alan Dershowitz, "Should Israel Have Agreed to Exchange Terrorists
   for a Kidnapped Soldier?" Huffington Post, *The Blog*, October 14, 2011,
   http://www.huffingtonpost.com/alan-dershowitz/should-israel-have
   -agreed_b_1011415.html.

6. "Text: Osama bin Laden," transcript of taped statement aired
   on Al-Jazeera, *Washington Post*, October 7, 2001, http://www
   .washingtonpost.com/wp-srv/nation/specials/attacked/transcripts
   /binladen_100801.htm.

7. John Nolte, "Helen Thomas Tells Jews 'Get the Hell Out of Palestine'
   and Go Back to Germany and Poland Disgraced White House Reporter
   Helen Thomas Dead at 92," Breitbart.tv, May 27, 2010 July 20, 2013,
   http://www.breitbart.com/Big-Journalism/2013/07/20/Disgraced
   -Journalist-Helen-homas-dead-at-92.

8. Theodor Herzl, "Author's Preface" in *Der Judenstaat (A Jewish State)*,
   trans. Sylvie d'Avigdor and Jacob De Haas (New York: Federation of
   American Zionists, 1917), http://en.wikisource.org/wiki/A_Jewish
   State%281917_translation%29/Front_Matter.

Chapter 10: The Spreading Wildfire

1 Blake Neff, "Historicity and Holy War: Putting the Crusades in
  Context," Dartmouth Apologia, The Augustine Collective, February
  2012, http://augustinecollective.org/augustine/historicity-holy-war-putting
  -the-crusades-in-context.

2. Robert Louis Wilken, *The First Thousand Years: A Global History of
   Christianity* (New Haven: Yale University Press, 2012), 307, 308.

3. Bat Ye'or, *Islam and Dhimmitude: Where Civilizations Collide* (Cranbury, NJ: Associated University Presses, 2002), 199.

4. Robert Spencer, "Iraq: We are Fighting for an Islamic State, says Al-Qaeda in Iraq," Jihad Watch, October 19, 2005, http://www.jihadwatch.org/2005/10/iraq-we-are-fighting-for-an-islamic-state-says-al-Qaeda-in-iraq.

5. Allan Hall, "Al-Qaeda Chiefs Reveal World Domination Design," The Age, August 24, 2005, http://www.theage.com.au/news/war-on-terror/alqaeda-chiefs-reveal-world-domination-design/2005/08/23/1124562861654.html.

6. Ishak Ibraham, *Black Gold and Holy War: The Religious Secret Behind the Petrodollar* (Nashville: Thomas Nelson, 1983), 20.

7. Brian J. Grim et al., "The Future of the Global Muslim Population: Predictions for 2010–2030," Pew-Templeton Global Religious Futures project, Pew Research Center, January 2011, http://www.pewforum.org/files/2011/01/FutureGlobalMuslimPopulation-WebPDF-Feb10.pdf.

8. "Zaid Shakir," DiscoverTheNetworks.org, February 2005, http://www.discoverthenetworks.org/individualProfile.asp?indid=974.

9. Robert Spencer, *Stealth Jihad: How Radical Islam Is Subverting America without Guns or Bombs* (Washington, DC: Regnery, 2008), 94.

10. Daniel Pipes, "The Danger Within: Militant Islam in America," commentary, DanielPipes.org, November 2001, http://www.danielpipes.org/77/the-danger-within-militant-islam-in-america.

11. Andres Tapia, "Churches Wary of Inner-City Islamic Inroads," *Christianity Today*, January 10, 1994, 36.

12. Mark S. Hamm, "Terrorist Recruitment in American Correctional Institutions: An Exploratory Study of Non-Traditional Faith Groups Final Report," commissioned report, sponsored by the National Institute of Justice, December 2007, https://www.ncjrs.gov/pdffiles1/nij/grants/220957.pdf.

13. Abdullah Saeed and Hassan Saeed, *Freedom of Religion, Apostasy and Islam* (Burlington, VT: Ashgate, 2004), 92.

14. Lawrence Wright, *The Looming Tower: Al-Qaeda and the Road to 9/11* (New York: Vintage, 2007), 261–62.

15. Ibid., 262.

16. Jan Goodwin, "Buried Alive: Afghan Women under the Taliban," *On the Issues*, Summer 1998, http://www.ontheissuesmagazine.com/1998summer/su98goodwin.php.

17. Terance D. Miethe and Hong Lu, *Punishment: A Comparative Historical Perspective* (New York: Cambridge University Press, 2005), 63.

18. Tim Butcher, "Saudis Prepare to Behead Teenage Maid," *Telegraph*, July 16, 2007, http://www.telegraph.co.uk/news/worldnews/1557628/Saudis-prepare-to-behead-teenage-maid.html.

19. "Public Debate in Saudi Arabia on Employment Opportunities for Women," The Middle East Media Research Institute, November 17, 2006, http://www.memri.org/report/en/print1793.htm.

20. Laura Bashraheel, "Women's Transport: Solutions Needed," *Arab News*, June 27, 2009, http://www.arabnews.com/node/325728.

21. Abdul Rahman Shaheen, "Saudi Women Use Fatwa in Driving Bid," *Gulf News*, June 20, 2010, http://gulfnews.com/news/gulf/saudi-arabia/saudi-women-use-fatwa-in-driving-bid-1.643431.

22. Bernard Lewis, *The Middle East: A Brief History of the Last 2,000 Years* (New York: Simon and Schuster, 1995), 227.

23. Ibid., 385.

24. Daniel Pipes, "Saudi Arabian Airlines Cleans Up Its Act," *FrontPage*, August 31, 2007, http://www.danielpipes.org/4878/saudi-arabian-airlines-cleans-up-its-act (see especially the August 31, 2008 update, which notes that the web page in question is sometimes taken down for "damage control," then reinstated later); Michael Freund, "Saudis Might Take Bibles from Tourists," *Jerusalem Post*, August 8, 2007, http://www.jpost.com/Middle-East/Saudis-might-take-Bibles-from-tourists; "International Religious Freedom Report for 2013: Saudi Arabia," US Department of State, July 28, 2014, http://www.state.gov/j/drl/rls/irf/religiousfreedom/index.htm?year=2013&dlid=222311#wrapper.

25. Amy Goodman, "A Growing Divide in Egypt: As Army Outlines Transition Plan, Brotherhood Vow Revolt after Massacre," transcript of video interview with correspondent Sharif Abdel Kouddous, Democracy Now! (blog), July 9, 2013, http://www.democracynow.org/blog/2013/7/9/a_growing_divide_in_egypt_as_army_outlines_transition_plan_brotherhood_vow_revolt_after_massacre.

26. Spencer Case, "How Obama Sided with the Muslim Brotherhood," *National Review Online*, July 3, 2014, http://www.nationalreview.com /article/381947/how-obama-sided-muslim-brotherhood-spencer-case; Raymond Ibrahim, "Egyptians Enraged by U.S. Outreach to Muslim Brotherhood," Middle East Forum, August 9, 2013, http://www .meforum.org/3578/us-outreach-egypt-muslim-brotherhood.

27. Hazel Haddon, Nada Hussein Rashwan, Randa Ali, Sherif Tarek, Salma Shukrallah, Bassem Abo El-Abbas, and Osman El-Sharnoubi, "Live Updates 2: Millions on Streets for Anti-Morsi Protests; 4 Dead in Upper Egypt," Ahram Online, June 30, 2013, http://english.ahram.org.eg /NewsContentP/1/75341/Egypt/Live-updates--Millions-on-streets -for-antiMorsi-pr.aspx.

28. Max Fisher, "Here's the Egyptian Military's Full Statement Warning It May Act in 48 Hours," *Washington Post*, July 1, 2013, http://www .washingtonpost.com/blogs/worldviews/wp/2013/07/01/heres-the -egyptian-militarys-full-statement-warning-it-may-act-in-48-hours/.

29. Jake Tapper, "Egyptian President Ousted by Military; Interview with Former Egyptian Army General Sameh Seif Elyazal," *The Lead with Jake Tapper*, CNN, July 3, 2013, http://transcripts.cnn.com /TRANSCRIPTS/1307/03/cg.01.html.

Chapter 11: A Spiritual Battle

1. Richard Kyle, *The Last Days are Here Again: A History of the End Times* (Grand Rapids: Baker, 1998), 27.

2. Ibid., 37, 44.

3. James R. McGovern, *The World of Columbus* (Macon, Georgia: Mercer University Press, 1992), 17.

4. Raymond Ibrahim, "Why Are Christians the World's Most Persecuted Group?," *Christian Post*, February 28, 2014, http://www.christianpost.com /news/why-are-christians-the-worlds-most-persecuted-group-115410/; "Study; Christians Are the World's Most Persecuted Religious Group, Catholic Online, February 10, 2014, http://www.catholic.org/news/hf /faith/story.php?id=54178.

5. Michael Carl, "Persecution of Christians on Rise—in U.S.," WND.com, September 17, 2012, http://www.wnd.com/2012/09 /persecution-of-christians-on-rise-in-u-s/.

Chapter 12: God's Peace Treaty

1. President George W. Bush, " 'Islam is Peace' Says President: Remarks by the President at Islamic Center of Washington, DC," White House press release, September 17, 2001, http://georgewbush-whitehouse.archives .gov/news/releases/2001/09/20010917-11.html.

2. "Bush: All Religions Pray to 'Same God,'" WND.com, October 7, 2007, http://www.wnd.com/2007/10/43906/.

3. Daniel Pipes, "Erdoğan: 'Turkey Is Not a Country Where Moderate Islam Prevails'," Daniel Pipes Middle East Forum, June 14, 2004 (updated September 1, 2014), http://www.danielpipes.org /blog/2004/06/erdo287an-turkey-is-not-a-country-where.

4. Jamie Glazov, "The Selling of 'Islam-Lite,'" FrontPage Mag, May 13, 2010, http://www.frontpagemag.com/2010/jamie-glazov/the-selling-of -%E2%80%9Cislam-lite%E2%80%9D/.

5. Daniel J. Flynn, *A Conservative History of the American Left* (New York: Crown Forum, 2008), 295.

6. "Give Peace a Chance," written by John Lennon/Paul McCartney; phonographic copyright (p) — Capitol Records, Inc.; copyright (c) — EMI Records Ltd.

7. Peter Neville, *Hitler and Appeasement: The British Attempt to Prevent the Second World War* (New York: Hambledon Continuum, 2006), 113.

8. Elizabeth Knowles, *What They Didn't Say: A Book of Misquotations* (New York: Oxford University Press, 2006), 86.

9. Robert Spencer, *Religion of Peace?: Why Christianity Is and Islam Isn't* (Washington, DC: Regnery, 2007), 79.

10. Dick Staub, "Why Don Richardson Says There's No 'Peace Child' for Islam," *Christianity Today*, February 1, 2003, http://www.christianitytoday .com/ct/2003/februaryweb-only/2-10-22.0.html.

About the Author

Michael Youssef was born in Egypt and lived in Lebanon and Australia before coming to the United States. He has degrees from Australia and the US, and he earned a PhD in social anthropology from Emory University. Michael served for nearly ten years with the Haggai Institute, traveling around the world teaching leadership principles. He rose to the position of managing director at the age of thirty-one, and his family settled in Atlanta.

Dr. Youssef founded The Church of The Apostles in 1987 with fewer than forty adults with the mission to "equip the saints and seek the lost." The church has since grown to a congregation of over three thousand. This church on a hill was the launching pad for *Leading The Way with Dr. Michael Youssef,* an international ministry whose weekly television programs and daily radio programs are broadcast more than 4,300 times per week in twenty-four languages to more than 190 countries.

For more on Michael Youssef, The Church of The Apostles, and *Leading The Way with Dr. Michael Youssef,* visit apostles.org and leadingtheway.org.

WORTHY
PUBLISHING

If you enjoyed this book, will you consider sharing the message with others?

- Mention the book in a Facebook post, Twitter update, Pinterest pin, blog post, or upload a picture through Instagram. Use hashtag #JesusJihadandPeace

- Recommend this book to those in your small group, book club, workplace, and classes.

- Head over to facebook.com/worthypublishing, "LIKE" the page, and post a comment as to what you enjoyed the most.

- Tweet "I recommend reading #JesusJihadandPeace by @MichaelYoussef // @worthypub"

- Pick up a copy for someone you know who would be challenged and encouraged by this message.

- Write a book review online.
  You can subscribe to Worthy Publishing's newsletter at worthypublishing.com.

WORTHY PUBLISHING
FACEBOOK PAGE

WORTHY PUBLISHING
WEBSITE